Great MARQUES

•STUART BLADON•CHRIS HARVEY•BRIAN LABAN•

Published in the United Kingdom by MMB,
an imprint of Multimedia Books Limited,
32-34 Gordon House Road, London NW5 1LP

Exclusive distribution in the USA by Smithmark Publishers Inc.,
16 East 32nd Street, New York, NY 10016

Managing Editor: Anne Johnson
Design: Megra Mitchell
Production: Hugh Allan

A catalogue record for this book is available from the British Library

ISBN 185375 162 6

10 9 8 7 6 5 4 3 2 1

Printed in Italy by Imago

Great MARQUES

- **BMW** -

- **FERRARI** -

- **JAGUAR** -

- **LAMBORGHINI** -

- **MERCEDES** -

- **PORSCHE** -

- **STUART BLADON** - **CHRIS HARVEY** - **BRIAN LABAN** -

C O N T E N T S

Below: *Frameless windows contribute to the attractively clean side profile of the 6-Series coupé body. This is a standard 635 CSi*

BMW

Stuart Bladon

Below: Special wheels and the discreet M badge with BMW Motorsport colors are among the few identity features of the high-performance M635 CSi, with four valves for each of its six cylinders

Contents

ENGINEERING EXTRAORDINARY

Perhaps because it is not tied up with the name of a founder, the early history of BMW is less clearly defined, and certainly less well known, than those of some of its older rivals. Its history has also been shaky, and more than once it has teetered on the verge of bankruptcy – a situation incredible to imagine now against the background of immense strength and enviable reputation.

Aero engines to autos

Although *Bayerische Motoren Werke* – the German name of the company – was founded in 1916 during World War I, it was not until 13 years later that BMW produced its first car.

The company started as the *Bayerische Flugzeugwerke*

AG (Bavarian Aircraft Company), with roots going back to 1913; and after the war, a biplane with a BMW engine designed by Dr Max Friz set an altitude record, reaching 31,826 ft. But there was not much demand for aero engines in those bleak years, and Friz and Franz-Joseph Popp, the company's chief engineers, looked eagerly for alternative outlets that would keep the firm in business.

Motor cycles seemed to offer the best hope. At first, BMW supplied engines for the Victoria-Werke motor cycle company in Nuremberg. Then the company acquired rights to build the Helios motor cycle and in 1923 produced its own design of motor cycle.

Attempts were then made to get into car production, and again the decision was taken first of all to tie up a production agreement to build an existing car. On 1 October 1928, BMW took over the Dixi-Werke, and their

little 3/15 model became the first car to bear the BMW emblem, from January 1929. The purchase of the Eisenach Vehicle Factory, which built the Dixi, gave BMW even more historic associations with the stumbling beginnings of the motor car, because the company had been founded by Dr Heinrich Ehrhardt as early as 1896, and the Dixi car dated back to 1904.

The Dixi had gone badly into decline, and had been saved by an extraordinary agreement with the British firm Austin, to produce under license a German version of their little two-seater runabout, the Austin Seven. The arrangement had proved immensely successful, and after the first 100 examples of the Seven had been shipped by rail from England in 1927, output in Germany built up spectacularly, and more than 6,000 were produced in 1928. A sure way to shock a BMW director is to remind him

Britain's famous Austin Seven was built under license by the Eisenach Vehicle Factory. When BMW took over, the little car, called the 3/15 hp Dixi, continued to be produced, and was the first car (opposite) to carry the BMW badge. Products developed rapidly in the 1930s – the Dixi grew into the 3/20 seen (left) in its 1934 form as the AM4, and the 315 sports (above) appeared in 1933

11

that his company's first adventure into car production was to build a little two-seater of English design!

Difficult times were to follow, with arrival of the depression in 1930. Improved versions of the Dixi were launched until it finally ceased production in January 1934.

The first true BMW design was the 303, launched in February 1933. It had a six-cylinder engine, and featured the 'double-kidney' design of oval radiator grille which has long been a recognition feature of BMW cars.

Rapidly the company began to evolve elegant body shapes with flowing wing lines; and the cabriolet became popular. Competition played an increasingly important part in promotion of the BMW image, and the 326, 327 and 328 enjoyed great success in motor sport in the 1930s.

With the arrival of war, production trickled on for a while, until May 1941. By the end of the war, the factory was in ruins, and it was a long time before the task of getting back to production could be tackled in earnest.

Post-war best seller

At the end of 1949, plans were underway to produce a new 2 liter six-cylinder saloon based on the earlier 326 model. It evolved into the 501, which first became available on the market in December 1952, with bodies hand-built by the coachbuilder Baur. Production reached a modest 1,645 cars in 1953, and 3,471 in 1954.

The 501 was a big car for a 2 liter engine, and a V8 had always been planned, which finally went into production as the 502 model in 1955. But of wider interest at that time was the introduction of the Isetta.

There was a boom in demand for small cars, and BMW had tied up agreement with the Italian firm ISO to build their strange little two-seater economy car with side-hinged door across the front. BMW's own single-cylinder 245 cc motor cycle engine was used, mounted at the rear, and driving twin close-coupled rear wheels.

Very inexpensive, the Isetta became for a while one of Germany's best-selling cars. It was called the 'rolling egg' and the Deutsche Bundespost (postal service) bought large numbers.

In 1956, engine capacity for the Isetta went up to 298 cc, and a much advanced version came out in 1957. Called the Isetta 600, it retained the front-opening door, had a side door as well, and the rear wheels were moved outward and independently mounted. A new horizontally-opposed twin cylinder engine was fitted.

There were high hopes for the revitalized Isetta; and it needed to be good, because sales of the big 501 and 502 models were falling disastrously. At the same time, development of a new and larger car started, using a design evolved by the Italian stylist Michelotti. It emerged in coupé and saloon form, using mechanical components derived from those of the Isetta 600. But by the time it reached the market, the BMW finances were in disarray, and the company hovered between collapse, financial rescue from various sources, and threats of take-over.

The 1500 arrives

The financial problems lingered on until 1961, when the car which was to reshape the destiny of the company emerged: the 1500. Although its engine capacity was only 1,499 cc, it was an extremely powerful little unit with overhead camshaft and inclined valves. The refreshingly clean-styled body introduced the 'forward-leaning' frontal profile which has characterized most BMWs ever since, and the car used a further development of the 700's independent rear suspension.

The 1500 was an immediate success. When they started to appear on German autobahns in 1963, people were staggered at the speeds which these sporty-looking cars could achieve. The pattern was set for the sports saloon which was to be the BMW *forte* in the years ahead.

It was followed by the more powerful 1800, and later came the adventure back into big car production, with the launch of the superb new 2500 and 2800 six-cylinder models.

A classic BMW was the two-seater 328 sports (opposite, top and left), built from 1936-40, which won many races; surprisingly few were built – only 461. Another historic BMW is this 303 model of 1934 (center, this page). It had a six-cylinder 1173 cc engine

Main picture and inset: The short-lived 335 model did not appear until late 1938, and only 410 were built before the war ended production in 1941. This fine 1939 example of the Cabriolet four-door (only 40 built) survives

BMW's first V8 car was the 502 of 1954
(below and opposite). Special-bodied
BMWs sharing the name Veritas are (lower
picture, this page) a 328, and (opposite) a
Veritas 507 prototype

Not quite the current concept of a BMW
but important in the company's history was
the little Isetta runabout (top); it had a front
door, and close-coupled rear wheels
(1955-62).
Above and opposite: The exciting Goertz-
designed 507 two-seater sports of 1956-59.
Right: The car that put the company back on
the road to success was the 1500 of 1962-64

TECHNICAL SUPREMACY

After its stumbling and uncertain beginnings, the BMW car soon achieved a reputation for being a well-engineered machine, promising good service, and using technical ingenuity to get optimum efficiency out of the fuel burnt. It has not just been a matter of developing good engines – the whole design of the car has played a part in this, and BMW's ability to keep surplus weight out of their cars has long been applauded.

In the past 30 years, which have seen the company climb steadily from relative obscurity to the position of one of the world's most respected makes, the importance of technical development has been exploited to the utmost. The design department has never lacked for ideas, nor has the engineering division proved lacking in carrying them through to fruition.

Technical progress became so rapid, with so much achievement to report, that BMW started holding an annual Technik Tag – a one-day conference for selected

motoring writers. Developments outlined at these annual meetings have later gone into production.

Computerized control

Examples include the development of anti-lock brakes, the car that decides for itself when it needs servicing, the on-board computer, and Motronics. Anti-lock brakes were developed by Bosch in conjunction with Daimler-Benz and BMW, and involve an electronic control system which detects when a wheel has stopped turning and sends a message to a central computer. A command then goes out to the pressure hydraulic system, momentarily interrupting the brake effort. The sequence goes through many times a second, and not only dramatically improves stopping distances on slippery surfaces, but also ensures that the car does not just spin into a wild skid, out of control.

At the introduction of the second-generation 5-Series in June 1981, BMW launched the service computer: it keeps count of the number of cold starts made, the type of running in terms of speeds and revs, and on a pre-programmed plan it determines when the car needs to be serviced, warning the driver by means of a diminishing number of green tell-tale lights. The car driven on a lot of stop-start work calls for itself to be serviced more frequently than one driven on long journeys at steady cruising speeds.

Since BMW first launched the on-board computer, to give instant readings of fuel consumption, distance travelled, average speed, and other calculations, many other makes have introduced their own versions. Nevertheless, the BMW on-board computer remains the most advanced of its kind, offering a complex range of

In good company: A 1938 328 owned by Miss Betty Haig with a 1956 Porsche 356 as stablemate

information and even providing a special way of thief-proofing the car. It was further improved in 1984 by provision of fingertip control for changing the read-out, so that the driver can see at a glance how speed, fuel consumption or any other aspect of a journey log is progressing.

Motronics

Motronics is the name given to an advanced engine management system, which again was developed by Bosch in conjunction with BMW. It appeared first on the 732i in 1980, and was later extended to other models. The system uses a computer which receives data from numerous sources, telling it, for example, what is the barometric pressure (significant when a car is climbing a mountain), the temperature of the coolant and of the ambient air, car speed, the engine revs, and the extent to which the driver is pressing on the accelerator. On the basis of this information, the computer determines how much fuel is to be injected into a given cylinder, and at what

memory to retain up to three combinations of reach and angle. All that the driver has to do, after someone else has driven his car, is press a button to resume his chosen seating position.

There is also the 'selectable' automatic. BMW recognize that styles of driving change according to mood, urgency, or traffic conditions, so they provide a switch near the selector for the automatic transmission of many models, which the driver can move to Sport or Economy, according to the level of automatic transmission response required. At Economy, the car loafs along in a very high top gear for effortless cruising, with the torque converter locked up to give positive drive above about 50 mph; but move the switch to S for Sport, and it immediately drops down to third and gives much more eager response. The control also provides a positive hold on third and second gears.

Effortless speed

BMW's ultimate technical achievement in production cars so far has been the 745i – a turbocharged version of the 735i. It is not only very fast indeed, but a car that is very forgiving, and is easy to drive fast. It goes without saying that the driver has to watch the speed carefully, because when he treads firmly on the accelerator he sends the speedometer needle scurrying round the dial towards 140 mph, with phenomenal and sustained acceleration. Driving the 745i with great care but using the performance to the full is to experience BMW technology at its most superlative.

millisecond the spark should be triggered.

The incredible thing about all this is that the calculations, following a predetermined engine 'map' programmed in advance for optimum efficiency in all conditions, are worked out afresh *each revolution.* This means that at 6,000 rpm, the computer must do its sums 100 times a second. But the system works marvelously, giving superb engine efficiency.

Another development which BMW featured is the refinement of having electrically adjustable seats with a

An early adventure into turbocharging was (opposite top) the 2002 Turbo. Opposite: The latest addition to the family – the M535i. Above: The little 700 LS Coupé of 1963. Left: Interior of a 735i which has 'memory' adjustment for its seats

The turbocharged engine of the 745i has an inter-cooler (below). Bottom: The elegant M635 CSi. Right: The M1 racing in Britain in the Procar series

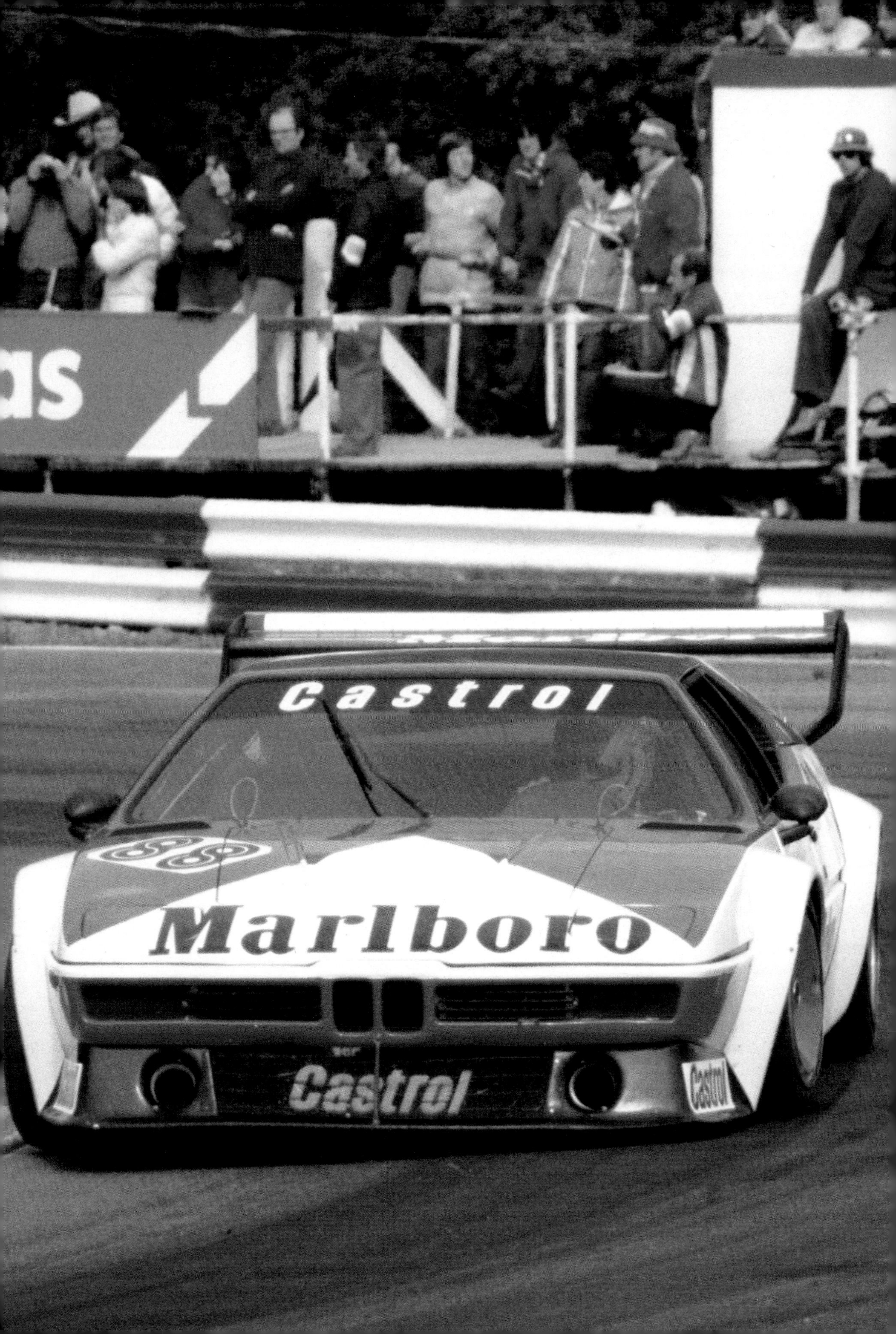
as
Castrol
Marlboro
Castrol
Castrol

Opposite: Imposing frontal view of a 635 Coupé, and (above) a 635 demonstrating the anti-lock brake system. Below, left: A 528i on the road in Germany, and (right) the magnificent 5-liter VC12 engine which appeared first in the 750iL

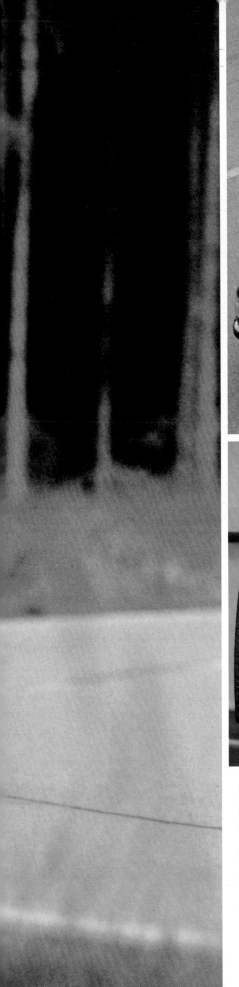

Previous pages: The 3-Series Convertible of BMW's own design – much tidier than the former Bauer conversion, which had a fixed roll-over bar.

Opposite: Tight cornering in the M635 CSi. This model range was replaced by the 8-Series in 1989.

Above: Turbocharged 7-Series, the 745i

SPORTING PROWESS

Even in the early Dixi days, the BMW has always been a car of sporting appeal, and inevitably the company's history is tied in with motorsport. In 1928 there were three little Dixis, with their tiny little drum brakes, flying round the Avus track, to take the first four places in the class for sports cars up to 1,000 cc.

Rallies, trials and races continued to play an important part in the company's activities, and with arrival of the 328 two-seater sports BMW had a very competitive car which dominated sports car racing from its mid-1936 introduction. Even after the war had started, the Mille Miglia was held in Italy in abbreviated form in 1940, and BMWs dominated the race, which was won by the coupé of von Hanstein/Bäumer.

Formidable competitors

After the war, BMW 328 engines were used to power many of the new racing cars, but it was to be some time before really competitive BMWs would be seen on the track again. Most significant efforts were the rally achievements with the little 700. The very fast 1500 and 1800 TI also set a worthy reputation for success in international rallies, where their good handling, low weight and generous power all helped to make them formidable competitors.

uschke von Hanstein and Walter Bäumer
on the 1940 Mille Miglia race; below is
e of the 1940 Mille Miglia cars, now in the
MW Museum at Munich.
ght: A 1937 Frazer Nash BMW

The real return to motor racing came with arrival of the lightweight coupé (see the chapter on the sporting coupé). Called the 3.0 CSL, it offered an impressive power/weight ratio, and in the right hands it proved a formidable contender in touring car races. First outing for the 3.0 CSL was at Monza in 1973.

The 2002 two-door saloon in ever faster and more modified form also became a significant force in production car races, usually with large flared wings to accommodate huge wheels and tires. There were also some impressive performances by the later 320i, made scarcely recognizable by the addition of fairings, air dams, wings and spoilers.

After a long period of very successful racing, the 3.0 CSL was eventually to be displaced by the new 635 CSi. In Group A racing form, the CSi's engine was developing 285 bhp at 6,100 rpm, and acceleration from standing start to 60 mph took only 6.1 sec. Top speed was over 180 mph.

The 1983 season was a memorable one for BMW, with Dieter Quester winning his fourth European Saloon Car Championship, while on a motor cycle Hubert Auriol had his second win in the Paris-Dakar rally. But of even greater significance was the success in Formula 1 racing: driving a Brabham with BMW turbocharged engine, Nelson Piquet became the first driver to win the championship at the wheel of a turbocharged car. He had three wins – Brazil, Monza and Brands Hatch (in the European Grand Prix). In the South African GP at Kayalami, the engine had its fourth win. Victory went to Riccardo Patrese.

BMW engines had enjoyed a great success in Formula 2 racing, winning a series of championships, and the decision had been announced in April 1980 that the company would supply Formula 1 engines, initially only for Brabham. The fascinating thing about the engine is that the cylinder block comes from a production car engine which has already seen service. Use stabilizes the metal.

The new Formula 1 engine had its first outing in January

1982, and won its first championship points in the following May, when Piquet was fifth in the Belgian GP at Zolder.

The fabulous M1

With a company like BMW, one can always be sure there will be still more spectacular cars in the future; but so far, the most exciting BMW of all time has undoubtedly been the M1. It looked fantastic, and it was.

The first public appearance of the M1 was at the Paris Show in October 1978, when it was announced that the necessary 400 examples needed for racing homologation would be built; and there were to be three versions – a road car, the 470 bhp Group 4 racing version, and the ultimate Group 5 racer with turbocharged 3.2 liter engine and some 850 bhp. The elegant coupé bodywork with gull wing doors was designed by the Italian specialist Giugiaro, and it was assembled under BMW Motorsport supervision at the Baur coachbuilding works at Stuttgart.

Development of the M1 was done by the Italian builder of exotic and very fast mid-engined cars, Lamborghini. The M1 was also mid-engined, with the six-cylinder twin ohc engine having four valves per cylinder and capacity of 3,453 cc, as for the production engine. Top speed was over 160 mph.

In various forms, the M1 starred at many international motor shows, but its most spectacular appearances were in what was known as the Procar series. A number of identical M1s would line up on the grid before major Grand Prix races, to be driven competitively in a free-for-all by the top GP drivers.

This had enormous spectator appeal; but with each car worth some £25,000, and all the costs of repairs and service to be faced, the expense was horrendous. Such is the price of publicity, but it shows also how far the once shaky little Bavarian assembler of English-designed two-seater runabouts has come, that it should be able to stage such a fabulous series of races to demonstrate its products.

Fore-runner of the M1, this is the striking BMW Turbo of 1972, now in the BMW Museum. Two examples were built, to give an insight into work being done by the experimental department

A remarkably effective publicity exercise was the BMW M1 – a mid-engined GT with 3453 cc six-cylinder twin ohc engine. Top speed was 162 mph. Racing versions were used in the Procar series of races, in the hands of GP drivers, before the Formula One race. Left: The 1980 Procar race at Monaco

Below: The M1 in racing. In the lower picture, the P. Neve/M. Korten car is seen at Le Mans in 1980. Opposite: On the grid for the 1980 Procar race at the British GP, at Brands Hatch; drivers are Marc Surer, Didier Pironi, Carlos Reutermann, Alan Jones and Hans Stuck

BMWs have established a formidable reputation for their performance in production saloon racing. Above: The 528i of Eddy Joosen/Hans Heyer lifts a wheel in anger, at Donington in 1982. Right: The warm-up lap at Donington. Opposite: Formula 1 racing with the Brabham-BMW. With a turbocharged BMW Formula 1 engine, Nelson Piquet won the Driver's World Championship in 1983 – the first of the turbo champions

THE SPORTS SALOON EVOLVES

Launch of the 1500 in 1961 not only put the company back on the road to financial recovery, but also set the pattern for the BMWs of the future. They would always be powerful, responsive and handle well; they would be true sports models, known in some quarters as 'thoroughbreds.' Soon after the 1500 came the more powerful 1800 model, launched at the 1963 Frankfurt Show.

It supplemented the 1500 as an additional model, and the engine was enlarged in both bore and stroke to give 1,773 cc capacity. Its maximum speed was just over 100 mph, against the 1500's 92 mph. Then came a twin-carburettor version – the 1800 TI – early in 1964.

Many people were disappointed to learn in March 1964 that production of the 1500, which had been greatly admired from its first arrival on the market, was to cease. But they need not have worried since its replacement was better still: the 1600. It had the same stroke as the 1500 engine, but used the larger bore and piston size of the 1800.

Major redesign of the 1800 engine, and increase of the bore diameter, pushed capacity to 1,990 cc, and the car was relaunched as the 2000, with revised appearance; later there was a better equipped version, the TI-Lux, which from 1968 was known as the 2000 tilux.

'Move over . . . to BMW'

New at the Geneva Show in March 1966 came an interesting addition to the range – a smaller car, with two-door body, and using the existing 1600 engine. It was warmly acclaimed in Europe and was the spearhead of a new drive to develop BMW sales in the United States. Two years later, a new version of the 1600 appeared with the 2000 engine, designated the 2002. With its compact size and low weight, the 2000 engine turned in an impressive performance and did much to build the reputation for the marque.

In Britain the 2002 was used in an aggressive marketing campaign which depicted it as seen in a driver's rear mirror, with the legend 'Move over'. The obvious implication was that one of these fast BMWs was catching up, and the driver should move out of the way; but the legend was then completed with the words '. . . to a BMW.' Later the same year, the launch of the 2500 and 2800 models brought a new large body style to the range, later to be fitted with even more powerful six-cylinder engines,

culminating in the 3.3 liter engine of the 3.3 Li. It ran in production for the short period 1976–7.

Another important introduction of the early 1970s was a turbocharged version of the 2002. Launched at the 1973 Frankfurt Show, it had special suspension, wider wheels and tires, and the turbocharged 2 liter engine could develop 170 bhp. Early versions had the name 2002 turbo written back to front on the forward apron, so that it read the right way round when seen in a driving mirror.

Much criticized, the cheeky legend was deleted from the front of the 2002 turbo after a short time, and the model itself was not to last long. With the oil crisis rapidly developing, 1974 was no time to be building an extravagant-sounding performance model; and production ended after less than a year.

Enter the 5-Series

In the saloon range there was clearly an over-large gap between the neat little 2002 and the large six-cylinder models, bridged only by successive versions of the

An early sporting BMW (opposite): the 326 of 1936-41. Above: Very fast in its day was the 2002ti (1968-71). Left: The 1500 body shell evolved into this sporting saloon – the 2000 in 1966; production continued until 1972

43

mid-range model whose body dated back to the 1500 of 1961. They were showing their age when, in 1972, a completely new mid-range saloon was launched: the 520.

Later, we were to come to refer to 'the 5-Series', as the number of models derived from the same bodyshell increased; but initially there was just the 520, with the well-tried four-cylinder 2 liter engine, and the 520i, with the advantage of fuel injection.

The body style pointed the way to the future evolution of BMWs, with slightly boxy shape, its continuation of the bumper line along the sides for lateral protection, and its hood extended out as a full width one-piece panel over the wing crowns. A six-cylinder 2½ liter model was launched in the following year, called the 525; and the range widened still more with the addition of another four-cylinder model

(the 1.8 liter 518 in 1974) and, in the following year, a luxury version with the six-cylinder 2.8 liter engine of the big cars, logically named the 528. July 1981 brought an up-dated and better shaped – but still very similar – body for the 5-Series as well; and the choice of models and engines increased impressively until by the end of 1984 all versions had fuel injection, capacity ranging from 1766 to 3430 cc; and there was also a very impressive turbo diesel version, the 524td, launched in 1983. The range was completed in November 1984 with the introduction of the four-cylinder 518i, and the effortlessly fast M535i with 3.4 liter six-cylinder engine.

Production of the small two-door model which had started as the 1600 was replaced in 1975 by a completely new body shell, again with just two doors, and called the

The larger and more aerodynamic 5-Series (above) was launched in 1988 to take the place of the much chunkier model seen (right) in its final form as the 528i. Above right: the Alpina 3.0SL racing in 1976

316, 318 and 320/320i. The appearance was very much that of a down-sized two-door 5-Series, and it was rapidly acclaimed as a worthy replacement for the much-loved 1602/2002 models. Highlight of the series was an all-new compact six-cylinder engine with belt-driven overhead camshaft, known as the M60 engine, in 1977.

At the beginning of 1983, the 3-Series came in for clever updating. The main body shell was retained and door pressings were unaltered, but clever reshaping of the front and rear metalwork achieved a more modern and slightly more aerodynamic look. The important news for many buyers was the four-door version which appeared at the Geneva Show in March. Another important extension of the 3-Series choice was the four-cylinder 1766 cc engine with fuel injection – the 318i.

Birth of the 7-Series

In steadily updated form, the big saloons of 1968 continued in production until 1977, when their magnificent replacement, the 7-Series, was launched. At first it came with a choice of three engine sizes – 2.8 and 3.0 liter, and 3.2 liter injection. Later came an advanced version of the 3.2 liter – the 732i – and then the 3.4 liter (735i), while the 2.8 liter became a fuel injected model as well, and hence graduated to 728i. This impressive range was topped off by the turbocharged version, known as the 745i; this was followed by V12 models, first the 750iL (long wheelbase) BMW 7-Series, launched at Paris 1986, and then the 750i standard wheelbase version at Geneva 1989.

*Left: The equivalent from the previous
5-Series, the M535i, launched in 1985.
Above left: The elegant 7-Series saloon.
Above: The V12-powered 750iL*

Above: The standard wheelbase V12 saloon, the 750i

Below: Nelson Piquet wins the 1983 World
Championship in a Brabham-BMW.
Bottom of the page: The very fast
turbocharged 745i

THE SPORTING COUPÉ

Carefully nurtured over the years, the image of BMW has always been that of a manufacturer of cars for enthusiasts and it is a foregone conclusion that there should always be that most sporting of cars – the two-door coupé – in the production line-up. Looking for a precedent, you could certainly say that the first car the company ever built – the little Austin-derived Dixi two-seater – was a sporty little car, even though we may now laugh at its lack of performance, brakes or roadholding.

Sporty styling

As the marque evolved in the 1930s, some elegantly sporting shapes emerged, of which perhaps the first notable one was the 303, launched in February 1933. The line-up included a sports two-seater of extraordinary

shape, with its headlamps recessed into the upper part of the radiator grille – though this feature was dropped by the time production started. The 303 was a handsomely styled coupé, worthy of the name of BMW.

One number, however, came to mean more than any other of the prewar BMWs: 328. It was launched in 1936, with open two-seater bodywork, curved wings with the headlamps built in for the first time, bonnet straps, and spats covering the rear wheels. The 328 was to stay in production for four years, and only 459 were built. It quickly established a fine record of successes in motor sport.

When struggling for revival after the war, BMW launched the 507 – a very sleek-looking open two-seater version of the 503, with detachable hardtop. It had a V8 engine, and the top speed was in the region of 125 mph. Introduced in 1956, it ran for three years. It was followed by the Bertone-designed 3200 CS, launched at the 1961 Frankfurt Show, and still with the V8 3.2 liter engine.

At a more realistic level than these exotic machines, there were also sporting coupé and convertible versions of the little BMW 700, which did much to salvage the failing position of BMW after its launch in August 1959. As there was no coupé derivative of the 1500 and later 1800 models, the little 700 had to fill the sporting role until its demise in 1964.

The performance version of the 328 Coupé had three carburettors for its 2 liter six-cylinder engine

In the following year, a strange-looking coupé emerged, with oblong headlamps built in at the corners, and using the same floor pan and running gear as the 2000 saloon. It was called the 2000 CS; there was also a less powerful version, the 2000 C. It proved very successful in spite of looks that were not to all tastes. Nearly 12,000 had been sold by the time production ended in 1969.

A much more elegant design was to follow: the six-cylinder CS, launched in September 1968. It had much more of what was then becoming recognized as characteristic BMW styling, with the flat bonnet deck, forward-leaning radiator grilles, and slender rear corner pillars. The new six-cylinder engine of 2.5 and 2.8 liter size had just been launched in the new big saloons, but the CS Coupé was offered initially only with the 2.8 liter unit, and was called the 2800 CS. Respected and very successful, the 2800 CS continued for three years, during which over 9,000 were built.

First important development for the CS was graduation to the new larger size of engine – with 3 liter capacity – and with choice of twin Zenith carburettors or Bosch fuel injection. The new model was named 3.0 CS or 3.0 CSi, according to engine type.

The expensive CSL

Special attention revolved around an additional model which appeared in the following year (1972), destined to put BMW back into the forefront of motor sport. It was the 3.0 CSL, looking much the same as a CS, but with lightweight bodywork making extensive use of aluminium, and fitted with wide rim alloy wheels.

It was appallingly expensive, but drivers could not help admiring its fabulous performance and enjoying its responsive character.

Several versions of the CSL were produced, the engine size creeping up to 3153 cc, and the power output reaching 206 bhp. It also became a formidable contender on the racing track.

Towards the end of its production span, the world plunged into the depths of the oil crisis, and as a gesture BMW launched an economy version of the Coupé, the 2.5 CS. However, demand for it was small and only just over 840 were produced.

To improve the aerodynamics of the CSL, wings and spoilers were added, and the version which emerged towards the end of the model's life was dubbed the Batmobile. It was not the sort of car you wanted to be in if stopped by the police for speeding. It looked as though it was going fast even when parked!

The new coupés

In 1976 the new coupé was called the Series 6 model, still retaining the key letters CS (standing for Coupé Sport); and there were two versions. You could have the 3 liter single carburettor model (630 CS), or there was an injection version with 3.3 liter engine (633 CSi).

This new BMW Coupé was altogether bigger, more businesslike and roomier, but still very much a sporting car. It also introduced a novel feature soon to be widely copied: a check control system, enabling the driver to confirm at the touch of a button that such services as the oil and windscreen washer levels are in order.

At the Frankfurt Show in 1983 came the crowning model: the M635 CSi. This fabulous machine has the same engine which had first appeared in the M1, with four valves per cylinder – a total of 24. The lower spoiler at the front, and the M badge on the boot lid, in the colours of BMW Motorsport, are the few outward signs that you are looking at one of the fastest cars on the road, capable of 159 mph, and acceleration from rest to 60 mph in 6.4 sec.

It was the last and best of the 6-Series, which continued until 1989, when the eagerly awaited 8 Series was launched, appearing first only in V12 form, as the 850i, launched at the Frankfurt Show. As well as introducing a new body style, the 850i brought many safety features, including seat belts mounted directly from the seats.

The 3.0 CSL in its final form, with wings and spoiler to improve aerodynamic performance

Opposite: Top of the BMW 6-Series coupé range, the M635 CSi, and (left) its interior with BMW Motorsport steering wheel. Another example of the M536 CSi is shown below, while the 3.0 CSL Batmobile is seen at the bottom of the page

Above: The new 8-Series coupé, launched
at Frankfurt 1989, initially only as the 850i
with V12 engine. Its top speed is
electronically restricted to 155 mph
(because of tyre problems at higher
speeds) and it accelerates from rest to
60 mph in 6.7 sec. Far right: a 635 CSi
without the Motorsport embellishments
and (right) the M1 mid-engined coupé

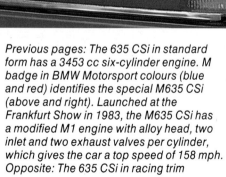

Previous pages: The 635 CSi in standard form has a 3453 cc six-cylinder engine. M badge in BMW Motorsport colours (blue and red) identifies the special M635 CSi (above and right). Launched at the Frankfurt Show in 1983, the M635 CSi has a modified M1 engine with alloy head, two inlet and two exhaust valves per cylinder, which gives the car a top speed of 158 mph. Opposite: The 635 CSi in racing trim

*Main picture: The M635 CSi at speed.
Inset: The M635 CSi (left) and the M1 from
which its highly developed engine is taken*

Below:
*Ferrari's continuing Formula One involvement
helped to breed cars as extraordinary as the F40*

FERRARI

Brian Laban

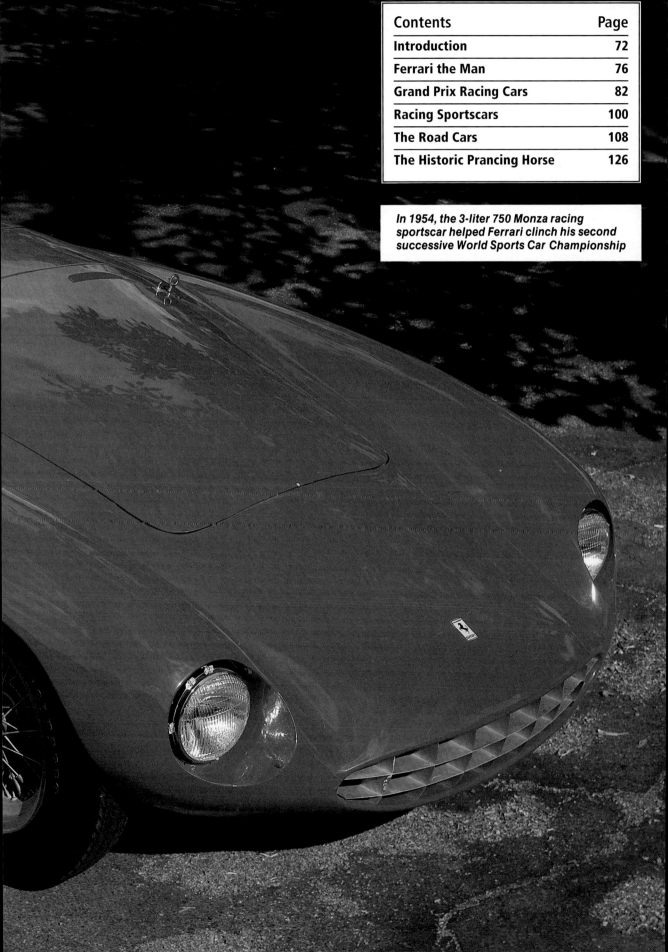

Contents

In 1954, the 3-liter 750 Monza racing sportscar helped Ferrari clinch his second successive World Sports Car Championship

INTRODUCTION

This is the story of one of the most famous names in motoring, a name synonymous everywhere with motor racing and the name on some of the world's greatest sportscars. This is the story of Ferrari.

It is not just the story of a great motoring marque, for Ferrari has only existed as a car manufacturer under its own name since 1947; it is also the story of Enzo Ferrari's unswerving dedication to motor sport – with the emphasis on sport – and to engineering excellence.

A passion is born

From humble beginnings, Enzo Ferrari carved a career in motor sport with Alfa Romeo in the 1920s which led to the formation of the racing team Scuderia Ferrari in 1929. With Alfa Romeo cars, and drivers of the caliber of Varzi,

Campari, Caracciola and the legendary Nuvolari, the Scuderia was one of the few serious challengers to prewar German superiority in Grand Prix racing. For two years from 1932, the Scuderia even included a motorcycle racing team that scored many successes, mainly with English-built Rudge machines.

In 1939, after a disagreement, Ferrari broke his Alfa ties and in 1940 he built his own first racing car. It was not called a Ferrari, that was not yet possible, but it sowed the seed. Soon after the war Ferrari built his next racing cars, and this time they *were* Ferraris.

First with sportscars and later in Grand Prix racing, formula two and in other fields of racing, Ferrari began to dominate. Now Ferrari has won more world drivers' championships and more constructors' championships

Just 200 examples of the turbocharged 1984 GTO (below) will be built initially, in a move to relaunch Ferrari into the front line of sportscar racing, where the marque first made its name. The racing success of the 1948 166 Spider Corsa (below right) started a demand for Ferrari competition cars for private entrants, such as Chinetti's 365GTB seen at Le Mans (right), which the GTO should continue into the 1980s. Ferrari's desirability to top class drivers does not stop on the track, and this Californian 250GT (bottom right), styled by Pininfarina, was once owned by Ferrari Grand Prix driver Peter Collins, tragically killed while racing for Ferrari in the 1958 German Grand Prix

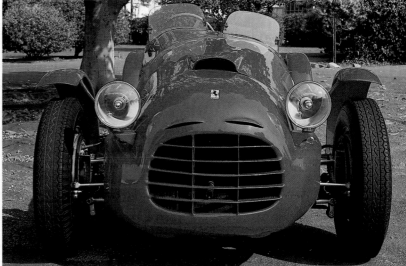

than any other marque. What's more, Ferrari's spread of success over so many years and through so many branches of motor sport – Grand Prix, sportscars, Formula Two, the mountain championships and the classic road races – is unique; and so it seems certain to remain.

Success and tragedy

From the start, racing success for Ferrari's works cars drew customers and Ferrari began to sell racing cars both in Europe and in America, where Briggs Cunningham bought the first example in 1949. Grudgingly at first, he also built a few cars for road use. His enthusiasm for them was limited to acknowledging their usefulness in financing his all-consuming passion for the sport. With time it mellowed into a deep pride in their uncompromising engineering and their unique charisma – but still as a means to another end.

Ferrari never compromised; in the 1960s, almost limitless Ford dollars could not buy his name, and later Fiat's far-reaching commercial involvement was accepted strictly on Ferrari's *own* terms. Ferrari retained control of his racing team, absolute control, and Fiat wielded the commercial muscle with a commendable sensitivity to the things that have made the Ferrari name great. A Ferrari, every Ferrari, is still a Ferrari.

This book is the story of that world, both the man and his cars. It traces Enzo's early years, the beginning of his ambitions, his cars' fantastic catalog of success. It is a story of tragedy as well as triumph, tragedy in Ferrari's dangerous sport and great personal tragedy. Ferrari always felt personally involved with his drivers and, inevitably, great drivers have died racing for Ferrari. Antonio Ascari's death in an Alfa Romeo in 1925 effectively led to the formation of Scuderia Ferrari, as Alfa played

down their official involvement with racing. Thirty years later, Antonio's son, Alberto, who had given Ferrari his first world drivers' championship, was killed while testing a Ferrari sportscar. Collins, Musso, Von Trips and Bandini all died racing for Ferrari, but in 1982 Enzo felt the death of Giles Villeneuve perhaps worst of all.

Pursuit of perfection

Ferrari raced on, not from callous indifference – very much the opposite. His commitment was almost religious – he knew what it was to lose an only son. When Dino died, at the age of 24 in 1956, Ferrari lost his heir apparent and perhaps a talented engineer-in-the-making. Dino's office at the Maranello factory was left untouched, virtually a shrine. A photograph took the place of the young man himself. Enzo emptied his heart of its secrets and doubts at Dino's graveside and the son was remembered in the Dinö

road and racing cars – badged not just with the prancing horse but with Dino's name.

The legacies of Ferrari's love of competition and pursuit of perfection are the magnificent cars in these pages.

In 1966, Ferrari failed to win the World Sports Car Championship for the first time since 1959, beaten by the might of Ford. Alongside the new 330P3 in 1966, Ferrari ran the small but beautiful Dino 206S (above left), forerunner of the Dino road cars. The 206S won no races but snatched second place in the fiftieth running of the classic Targa Florio road race. The Dino was one of the few Ferraris not to carry the Prancing Horse shield as seen on the Daytona (top) and on Arnoux's car in the 1984 British GP (above)

FERRARI THE MAN

Enzo Ferrari was born in the small northern Italian town of Modena in February 1898, the son of a metalworker. The young Ferrari's ambitions however were not in his father's metalworking business, but as an opera singer or as a sports journalist – until September 1908 when his father took him to see Nazzaro's Fiat win the Targa Bologna road race. From that day he knew that he wanted to be a racing driver.

First taste of the track

In the winter of 1918, after long periods in hospital, he was invalided out of the Italian army, where he had served first as a blacksmith in the artillery and later as an aero engine mechanic. His father and his elder brother had both died during the war and Enzo did not re-open the family business. Instead, through a friend, the racing driver Ugo Sivocci, Ferrari found a job as a test driver for the small sportscar manufacturer CMN, in Milan. In October 1919 h had his first race for his new employers, at the Parma Poggio di Berceta hillclimb, where he finished fourth.

He left CMN in 1920 to join Alfa Romeo and in October he finished second for Alfa in the Targa Florio, the classic Sicilian road race.

As well as driving and testing Alfa's racing cars, Ferrari also brought in new engineering and design talent, including the legendary designer Vittorio Jano from Fiat, which helped Alfa's racing program to forge ahead.

Ferrari's own racing career was short and of no great

impact. He scored his share of relatively minor wins but he was still dogged by ill health and, in 1924, by a nervous breakdown which stopped him racing in the Lyons Grand Prix. He finally (and perhaps not too reluctantly) retired from racing in January 1932 after the birth of his only son, Dino, the greatest and most tragic influence in his later life.

Recognition and independence

Although he was never famous as a driver, Enzo's contribution to racing, even before his later fame as a manufacturer, was considerable; in 1928 he was given the title *Commendatore*, a title which he gladly relinquished when honors awarded by the Fascist government were reviewed after the war. Now he is happy to be called Ferrari.

In December 1929 Enzo left Alfa and founded Scuderia Ferrari. Although officially independent, it was in effect the Alfa works racing team. In 1938 Ferrari rejoined Alfa officially, as head of the new Alfa Corse team, but within a year, after he had argued with one of Alfa's own engineers, he left to found his own company, Auto Avio Construzione,

which was soon to become a racing car manufacturer. In 1940, unable to use his own name because of his Alfa severance conditions, Ferrari called his first two cars '815s'.

The first car to be called a Ferrari appeared after the war, in a minor sportscar race in May 1947, and the company was renamed Auto Avio Construzione Ferrari. The first race win followed in the same month. As the marque quickly became established in competition (and shortly afterward started selling cars for both road and track), Ferrari was happy to see his beloved son Dino, already showing promise as an engineer, becoming his natural successor. Then in June 1956, and after a long illness,

A man and his cars: Enzo Ferrari confers (below left) with Achille Varzi at the wheel of one of the Scuderia's Alfa Romeo P3 racers, one of the classic designs which Ferrari helped to fruition. Almost forty years later, a 1969 365GTB4 leads the pack in the 1983 'Ferrari Days' meeting in Italy (below)

Dino died. Before his death he had worked with Jano on the new V6 racing engine for 1957 and his name is remembered on many subsequent Ferrari V6 and V8 engines. The Imola Grand Prix circuit in Italy is also named the Circuit Dino Ferrari in his honor.

Ideals – not big deals

Enzo went to see the first Dino model race, but in later years rarely went to Grand Prix events. He controlled his team from his office, but with just as firm a hand. His closest approaches to the racing cars which bore his name were in the clinically spotless racing workshops and, on rare occasions, at the company's superb Fiorano test track. Here, Ferraris of all types continue to be tested on a modern circuit which reproduces characteristics of race

tracks all over the world, closely analyzed by the most sophisticated electronic equipment. Although Ferrari accepted the technical complexity and, to some extent, the big money politics of modern Grand Prix racing, he never accepted overpowering commercial sponsorship from outside the motor industry. He proudly continued to race his cars in the Italian national racing color, red.

In 1969 Ferrari signed over control of Ferrari production to the giant Fiat empire. Although he relinquished the cut and thrust of day-to-day car building, he was not unhappy. Fiat agreed to support Ferrari's racing program with full and continuous sponsorship and Ferrari continued to control his racing team until his death in 1988.

In 1952 Ferrari replaced twelve cylinders with four in the 2-liter 500 (top right), with which Alberto Ascari won the Formula 2 based World Championship – Ferrari's first. This was one of the few years in which F2 cars competed for the World title, but Ferrari later achieved great success in F2 proper. The 1969 Tasman Dino (above right) with which Chris Amon won the Australian and New Zealand winter series, developed from the V6 Dino. Ferrari has built almost every size and shape of engine: contrasting with the four-cylinder 500 and the V6 Dino are the V12 engined 1948 166 Corsa (above) and the midgoing V8 engined 308GTS (right), of which this is a 1978 example

SEN 888S

It took Ferrari (inset opposite) a long time to warm to building road cars, but today even cars like the Boxer (main picture) are built on a production line

THE GRAND PRIX RACING CARS

In the light of his background with the Alfa Romeo Grand Prix team up to the Second World War, it was not surprising that Enzo Ferrari was quickly drawn to the top level of motor sport when he became a manufacturer himself.

Although earlier Ferrari cars were entered in events loosely called 'Grand Prix', the first real formula one Ferrari, the 125 Gran Premio, appeared in the Italian GP at Valentino Park, Turin, in September 1948. Three of the V12 cars were entered and Raymond Sommer scored an encouraging third place in the only one to finish. The 125 GP won next time out, at Lake Garda, and in 1949 modified

125s won the Swiss and Czech GPs, the *Daily Express* Trophy at Silverstone and the European GP at Monza. Also in 1949, the British industrialist Tony Vandervell bought a 125 that he modified as the first Thinwall Special – the predecessor of his own Vanwall.

1950 was the first year of the official world championship for drivers, but Ferrari were well beaten by Enzo's old team Alfa Romeo. In 1951 Ferrari finally beat Alfa, when Gonzalez won the British GP, and in 1952, with new four-cylinder 500 cars, Ferrari won their first world championship as Alberto Ascari won all six GPs that he

tarted. In 1953 he won five more and was champion gain, but in 1954 Ferrari was totally outclassed by the eturn of Mercedes-Benz.

The 1955 cars, known as Super Squalos or Sharks, vere equally ineffective and in 1956 Ferrari took over evelopment of Lancia's D50 cars. Financially troubled ancia withdrew from racing when Ascari, now *their* top river, was killed while testing a sports Ferrari. Part of the akeover, organized by the Italian Automobile Club, was a ve-year grant to Ferrari from Fiat. In 1956 the Ferrari-nodified Lancia driven by Fangio won the championship.

he problem years

y 1957 the cars were more Ferrari than Lancia but didn't in a single GP. For 1958 Ferrari ran the Jano-designed V6 ino 246s, developed from the formula two design on vhich his late son had worked. With this car Mike Hawthorn ecame the first English world champion, only to die in a pad accident shortly afterward.

Ferrari's next world champion was also the first

American to win the title, when Phil Hill won with the rear-engined V6 Type 156. Sadly, Hill's team-mate Wolfgang von Trips was killed at Monza in an accident which also killed 14 spectators.

With the sudden emergence of the British Grand Prix teams such as Cooper, BRM, Lotus and Brabham, Ferrari had a lean time through the rest of the 1 ½ liter formula of the early 1960s, cheered up only by John Surtees' championship in 1964.

Ferrari's fortunes were little better through the early years of the new 3 liter Grand Prix formula, in spite of starting with a new V12 design in the Type 312. Surtees left

Tony Vandervell's Thinwall Special *(below left) was one of a series of much modified Ferraris which paved the way to his own successful Vanwall GP cars. While Vandervell developed the* Thinwall *in 1952, Ferrari was winning the Championship with the* 500 *(below and bottom)*

the team and Bandini was killed in a fiery accident at Monaco in 1967. In spite of the efforts of drivers including Jacky Ickx, Chris Amon and Clay Regazzoni, Ferrari struggled as badly as Lotus, Tyrrell, Matra and McLaren dominated the championship and the new Ferrari flat-12 engine failed to back its potential with results. Ferrari could win races but simply could not take the championship.

Niki Lauda put Ferrari back on top in 1975 with the 312T and might have won again in 1976 but for the horrific accident at Nurburgring which almost claimed his life. Ferrari did win one of his eight constructors' cups in 1976 and Lauda confirmed his return in 1977 by winning the drivers' championship once again.

The South African Jody Scheckter gave Ferrari his ninth drivers' championship in 1979, with the development of the flat-12 312, but then Ferrari began to struggle again. In the early 1980s Ferrari began to develop their turbocharged V6-engined GP car but its prodigious power was wasted on a chassis whose handling was unpredictable in inexperienced hands and often bordered on the dangerous.

Back on top

By 1982, however, it seemed that Ferrari was back, as Canadian Gilles Villeneuve and Frenchman Didier Pironi dominated the championships – before suffering tragic accidents. Many teams would not have survived such mortal blows, but Ferrari fought back, developing incredibly powerful turbocharged cars for drivers like Patrick Tambay and René Arnoux, followed by Michele Alboreto. As the British McLaren team dominated the world championships, the Austrian Gerhard Berger and Briton Nigel Mansell took normally-aspirated Ferraris back to the top as race-winners. It needed only the signature of McLaren team leader and multi-world champion Alain Prost as Mansell's team mate for 1990 to give the marque new hope of world championship victories.

Ferrari's World Champions have come from all over the world. Mike Hawthorn, seen (above) on his way to winning the 1954 Spanish GP, became the first Englishman to win the World title, in 1958. Phil Hill, shown here (top right) just before retiring his battered Dino 246 from the 1960 French GP, took the title to America in 1961. Ascari drove the 500 (above right) to the World title for Italy, briefly interrupting the Argentine Juan Manuel Fangio's still unbeaten run of five championships. Jody Scheckter, pictured (right) in his 312T4 in the pits at the 1979 Belgian GP was the first – and so far only – South African World Champion, in that year. Ferrari may be fiercely and proudly Italian but his winners are totally cosmopolitan!

Californian Phil Hill joined the Ferrari GP team in 1958 and won his first GP, the Italian, at Monza, in 1960. In 1961 he won the World Championship, but sadly after his team-mate, Wolfgang von Trips, had been killed in Italy. After the championship win of 1961, 1962 was a disastrous year for Ferrari and Hill is seen here on his way to retirement with the 'shark-nose' 156 from the British Grand Prix

Ferrari's GP drivers have had peculiarly mixed fortunes. John Surtees, a brilliant engineer and test driver, here in the 1965 Dutch GP (left) where he finished seventh, added the four-wheeled championship in 1964 to numerous two-wheeled world titles. New Zealander Chris Amon, here with the 312 in the 1969 Spanish GP (top) was undoubtedly gifted, but perhaps the unluckiest man in racing and time and again certain victory melted away. Mario Andretti on the other hand won his first ever GP for Ferrari, the 1971 South African race, with the 312B, before switching to the newer 312B2, in which he is shown (above) heading for fourth place in Germany

Niki Lauda won two championships for Ferrari, in 1975 and 1977, and might have made it three in a row but for his terrible accident in 1976. After his remarkable recovery he scored eighth place in the Canadian GP (above left) but then retired his same 312T2 from the rain soaked Japanese GP (left), the last of the season, narrowly losing the title to James Hunt. The talented young Italian Nanni Galli finished thirteenth on his only outing for Ferrari, with this 312B (above) in the 1972 French GP. Only two Italians have driven Ferrari GP cars since then, Merzario and now Michele Alboreto

This picture of Scheckter in an unclothed 312T4 (far left) in 1979 gives some idea of the complexity and compactness of the modern GP car. When Canadian Gilles Villeneuve joined Ferrari in 1977 he had several unfortunate early accidents but his natural brilliance eventually matured and during 1979 (above) he led the championship for a while, but, sadly, he would never win it. Carlos Reutemann won the British GP in 1978 (left) with the 312T3 but Ferrari lost the title to Lotus, the only team to challenge their incredible GP record. Carlos Reutemann won the British GP in 1978 (left) with the 312T3.

Two very different views of the GP spectacle at two apparently similar but really remarkably dissimilar circuits, Long Beach in California, and Monaco. Jody Scheckter was airborne and fighting hard with the 312T5 (left) in the streets of Long Beach in 1980 and Gilles Villeneuve was equally unhappy with the evil-handling 126C turbo car at Monaco the following year (above). Both Monaco and Long Beach are street circuits, but Monaco has a history going back to the early days of racing and Long Beach was a relatively short-lived newcomer. Wherever the circuit, Scheckter and Villeneuve would both have agreed at the time that the GP Ferrari's incredible power was largely wasted on a very poor chassis, but neither of them ever gave up trying

The thirsty turbocharged cars with their appetite for soft tyres brought a new sight (or at least the return of an old one) to GP racing in 1982 and 1983 – pit stops. This is René Arnoux refuelling as his tyres are changed during the 1983 German GP

Buderus-Ecomatic
Juno
Agip
28
MAGNETI MARELLI
GOOD YEAR
BOXEN

Rarely has a foreigner been more popular in a
Ferrari team than the Briton Nigel Mansell,
despite the Union Jack on his helmet. Against
all the odds, he won his first race for what
amounts to the Italian national team in Rio de
Janeiro in 1989, and then went on to take
second place to world championship leader
Alain Prost in the British GP. Here we see him
refuelling during the Brazilian GP (left) and
again during the British GP (top). Mansell was
delighted when Prost decided to move over
from the British team to join him at Ferrari; he
said he felt Prost was one of the few drivers
who could teach him anything

RACING SPORTSCARS

The first car that Ferrari ever built was a racing sportscar, but it was not called a Ferrari. When Ferrari left Alfa Romeo in 1939 and founded his own company he was banned from using his own name on a car for four years; nevertheless, in 1940 he did build two eight-cylinder cars (one of them for Alberto Ascari) and they raced in the Brescia GP in April, entered as 815s. Both led their class, but both retired.

No more 815s were built because of the war (during which Ferrari moved from Modena to nearby Maranello under decentralization laws), but at least Ferrari was free to use his own name on the cars he now planned to build. The first Ferrari proper, the V12 engined 125 Sport, was announced in 1946 and appeared for the first time in a sportscar race at Piacenza in May 1947, driven by Franco Cortese. He led the race but failed to finish. The first sportscar win came two weeks later when Cortese won a race in Rome. Nuvolari and Sommer also won for Ferrari in 1947 and soon Ferrari was developing his sportscars with larger engines and improved chassis, derivatives of the 166 lasting from 1948 to 1953.

Classic Wins

Ferrari sportscars soon began to win the classic races. In 1948 Biondetto won the Mille Miglia (after which the 166 Mille Miglia model was introduced) and the Targa Florio, repeating both wins in 1949. That year also saw Ferrari's first win in the greatest of all sportscar races, Le Mans, and

Briggs Cunningham won at Watkins Glen with the first car imported into the USA.

Ferrari won the Mille Miglia again in 1951 on the debut appearance of the larger engined 340, which later gave way to the 4.5 and 4.9 liter types 375 and 375 Plus. In 1951 Taruffi and Chinetti won the grueling near-2000-mile Carrera Panamericana with a 212 Inter, which led Ferrari to build specifically American types such as the 340 Mexico and 342 America.

Reigning champions

Ferrari won the world sports car championship for the first time in its inaugural year, 1953, and they won the championship again in 1954, also adding another Le Mans victory. In fact between 1953 and 1961 Ferrari lost the world sports car championship only twice, to Mercedes-Benz in 1955 and to Aston Martin in 1959. They won the all-important Le Mans race in 1958 and every year from 1960 to 1965, with cars such as the 250 Testa Rossa

(named for its red valve covers), the 330P, 250P and the classic 250LM.

In the early 1960s Ford had ambitions to win at Le Mans to promote their new sporting image and they tried very hard to buy into Ferrari as a short-cut to winning the race, but Ferrari resisted and took great delight in holding off the Ford steamroller until 1966. Sadly, 1965 was Ferrari's last win at Le Mans as first Ford then Porsche, Renault and Matra began to dominate the race. Ferrari's nine wins in

Of all Ferrari's racing sportscars, perhaps the most illustrious is the 250GTO – the letters standing for Gran Turismo Omologato, *homologated strictly for racing. The GTO is not only an effective car but also a beautiful one (below left). It probably looks at its best of course as here (below) in the classic Sicilian mountain scenery of the 1964 Targa Florio road race. This is Norinder's and Troberg's Swedish entered car on its way to ninth place*

Motor racing is a noisy, smelly sometimes dangerous sport, but it does have its beauty. There is the unquestionable beauty of the engineering of the V12 engine in the rear of the 1967 330P4 racing sportscar (top left), the car with which Ferrari won that year at Daytona and at Monza in Italy. There is the beauty of the slippery, aerodynamic lines of the 206SP Dino sportscar (above) an incredibly functional form. There is also a certain beauty in the settings – as with Jacky Ickx's 312P (one of the most successful racing sports prototypes ever, which won every race it entered in 1972) emerging from the gloom of the Belgian forest with headlamps ablaze during the 1972 Spa 1000km classic (left). The Muller/Williams 275LM sweeping through the Esses during the 1968 Le Mans 24-hour race just as the sun begins to set (above left).

the 24-hour classic would not be equalled by Porsche until 1984.

In 1957 Taruffi won the last running of the Mille Miglia with a type 335. Ferrari racing sportscar development continued to follow closely on the Grand Prix cars, with V6 engines alongside the superb V12s and rear engines from the early 1960s.

Changing with the times

From 1961 the format of the sportscar championship varied considerably: sometimes it was run as a GT championship, later as a series for marque prototypes. Ferrari won each of the GT style championships from 1962 to 1964, and won the first prototype championship in 1965 before bowing to the might of Ford and Porsche until 1972.

That was a spectacularly successful year for the team, and it introduced the 312P, closely based on the Grand Prix car of that year. The 312Ps won every race they entered, taking the championship by a massive margin, but strangely they were not raced at Le Mans.

In 1973 Ferrari was beaten both at Le Mans and in the championship by Matra who took over the competitive edge. It was Ferrari's last year as a serious works competitor in sportscar racing and Ferrari colors have mostly been carried since by various privately entered racing versions of road cars such as the Daytona and Boxer – honorably, though with little chance of outright success against the purpose-built racing cars which now contest the endurance racing championships.

It seems appropriate that the Ferrari road cars keep the marque in sportscar racing; the sports racers developed from the Grand Prix cars and the road cars owe much to the racing sportscars. With Ferrari, racing really improved the breed.

Phil Hill began his association with Ferrari through the racing sportscars and won Le Mans for Ferrari in 1958, 1961 and 1962 – each time with Olivier Gendebien. His relaxed style and precise line are beautifully shown in this study of him with the Testa Rossa in the 1959 Tourist Trophy race, at Goodwood in England

1970 was not a particularly good year for Ferrari in the Sports Car Championship, with only one win to show – for Vaccarella, Giunti and Andretti, in the USA at Sebring. Vaccarella and Giunti also took fourth in Belgium (left), the American pair Sam Posey and Ron Bucknum were fourth in a wet Le Mans (top) and Mike Parkes and Herbert Muller were a disappointing thirteenth in Britain (above) with Scuderia Filipinetti's privately entered 512S

THE ROAD CARS

Once Enzo Ferrari started to build his competition cars, particularly his racing sportscars, it was probably inevitable that a demand would arise for Ferraris for the road, and it arose very quickly. Ferrari himself, however, was far more concerned with his fledgling racing team and at first was almost totally uninterested in building cars for the road. He soon had to recognize the demand, and of course selling cars would bring some much needed finance for the increasingly expensive racing development. Yet when Ferrari built his first road cars he built them with little or no concern for efficient production, laying them down in batches, typically, of only half a dozen, of which any two were seldom identical. Only later did he put road car production onto anything approaching an orderly basis.

The first road car was the 166 Inter, a direct descendant of the race-winning V12 166 Mille Miglia, which went on sale in 1947 in a variety of body styles from cycle-winged austerity to coachbuilt beauty. It grew up into the larger-engined 195 and 212 Inters and finally the short chassis 212 Export.

First US models

Perhaps 250 of the various 166 derivatives were built and these included the first car specifically for the American market, the 200 bhp 342 America. This led to the larger-engined 375 of 1953, the 1955 410 Superamerica and eventually to the rapid 410 Superfast.

By 1953 the cars were becoming civilized road cars rather than thinly disguised racers and the introduction of

PFP 1

the 250 Export and Europa showed a recognition of the road cars' importance. The 250 Europa was the first real effort at a GT car which could be built in worthwhile numbers and from it Ferrari developed his first 'standard' road car, the 250 GT, with coachwork options from the likes of Pininfarina, Scaglietti and Zagato. It was also available in Berlinetta form – literally 'little saloon' – but in Ferrari terms a lightweight version of the coupé, mainly for racing in the new world championship which now catered for 'roadgoing' GT cars.

The sensational 1962 250 GTO was the ultimate short-chassis performance development of the 250 series – this one unashamedly for racing. The series also included the more practical 1961 250 GT 2+2, the first Ferrari with more than two seats, and the beautiful 250 GT Lusso. With a larger engine, the 250 became known as the 330 GT, and became particularly popular in the USA.

Power, performance, good styling

From 1964 the 275 GTB and the open 275 GTS (S for Spyder) took production methods a step further, with virtual standardization of body style and a much improved chassis far more in keeping with road requirements.

In 1968 the 275 GTB4 was replaced by the pinnacle of the front-engined roadgoing Ferraris, the magnificent 175 mph 365 GTB4 Daytona, styled by Pininfarina and one of the fastest road cars ever made. Later the Daytona was supplemented by the even more desirable drophead 365 GTS4 Daytona Spyder – the ultimate wind-in-the-hair car.

As well as catering for ultimate performance, Ferrari also looked after a different sector of the market from 1968. He

Ferrari's early road cars didn't look too much different from some of his racing sports cars, but with Ferrari usually only being interested in the mechanics there was room for some imagination from the coachbuilders. The very simple 1947 166 Inter (below) was one of Ferrari's first real road cars. The very pretty Vignale bodied drophead 212 of 1949 (bottom) was basically a bigger engined derivative, as was the 1951 212 Barchetta, or 'little boat' (below left)

introduced the smaller and truly mass-produced Dino 206 GT – badged at first not by the prancing horse but simply with the name of Ferrari's lost son. Not only did the Dino put Ferrari into the Porsche part of the market, but it also introduced his production cars to the Grand Prix style mid-engined layout, with engines produced to Ferrari specifications by Fiat. The Dino series developed through the more powerful 246 GT and the open 246 GTS of 1972. Ferrari later sprang a surprise with the 308 GT4, which had a V8 engine in place of the V6 usually associated with Dino's name, and a body styled by Bertone rather than Pininfarina; it was not universally well received. Before long, Ferrari brought Pininfarina style back with the pretty 308 GTB and GTS. These were followed by the more powerful 328 and 348 series.

Reflecting the Grand Prix and sports racing cars, Ferrari inevitably adopted the mid-engined layout for his road

cars. In 1971 he revealed the first 'full-size' mid-engined road car in the stunning Berlinetta Boxer; like its Grand Prix contemporaries, it used a beautiful and potent flat-12 engine. The first Boxer had a 4.4 liter engine but by the early 1980s this had grown to a full 5 liters, keeping the Ferrari name in the forefront of the fastest cars in the world, ultimately developing into the new Testa Rossa.

Ferrari also catered for those who needed a full four-seater performance car with the elegant Pininfarina-designed 400, which offered not only four seats but also an automatic transmission.

In mid-1984 Ferrari underlined his commitment to ultimate performance with the announcement of a new 189 mph road car bearing a famous Ferrari name, the GTO – another new claimant to the title of fastest road car in the world, and every inch a Ferrari, before it was supplemented by Ferrari's last car, the F40.

The word Berlinetta, literally, means a small
sedan, but in Ferrari's terminology from the
mid-1950s it came to mean the lightweight
version, often for racing, of any of Ferrari's
coupés. At first however, as with the 1950
195 Berlinetta (above), which was the larger
engined successor to the 166, the
designation simply meant coupé. Especially
in the early 'production' years, racing
connections were never forgotten for long,
with touches like the bonnet straps on this
195 Spider (above right) – and the 1950
166MM road car (inset) took its name from
Ferrari's first win in the Mille Miglia road
race, scored in 1948. Even in the 1970s and
80s, beautiful, functional design as on this
1971 365GTS/4 Daytona Spider (right) left no
doubt about Ferrari's racing background

One of the most spectacular roadgoing Ferraris was this 250LM, or Le Mans, a thinly disguised coupé version of the 250P racer, built in limited numbers to secure homologation for the newly introduced GT racing class – which it failed to do. Less like all-out racers, but equally stirring, were some of the cars for the American market, usually the fastest and biggest engined variants. Shown here (insets, left to right) are the 1952 340 Mexico (named for Ferrari's victory in the Mexican Road Race), Pininfarina's 1958 410 Superamerica, and this stunning Pininfarina design on a 1956 410 Superamerica chassis, the first Superfast

Variations on the 250 theme during the first true production series' long run were numerous and mostly very desirable. The 1962 short chassis 250GT SWB Berlinetta (far left) was the immediate precursor of the classic racing 250GTO, designed by Ing Bizzarini. On the 'standard' chassis length were the beautiful 250GT Lusso – literally 'luxury' (left) and the 1963 250GT California, both styled by Pininfarina (below)

Chassis development took a step ahead
with the 275GTB, launched in 1964 as
successor to the 250GT Lusso and of which
this is a 1967 model. On the 275GTB the V12
engine was at the front and the gearbox
was at the rear, for better weight
distribution. The registration number is
highly appropriate for this 1965 500
Superfast (inset), the most powerful and
probably the fastest production car of its
day and last of the specifically 'American'
models

The 1965 330GT (far left) was, in effect, the 250GT 2 + 2 with a larger, 4-liter V12 and a five-speed gearbox. It was also Ferrari's largest car at the time and available as a coupé or Spider. At the other end of the size scale, Ferrari offered the Dino series, introduced with the 1968 206GT model (below) as a larger scale production operation aimed right at the Porsche 911 market sector. The car was styled by Pininfarina, developed from the 206S racer and with a Fiat-built V6 engine. Instead of the Ferrari name it simply carried 'Dino' badges. A V8 engine was introduced in the Bertone styled 308GT but Pininfarina was brought back to style the lovely 308GTS Spider (left) introduced in 1977 and of which this is a 1978 example. The coupé version of the car, the 308GTB was remarkable in its 1975 introduction in bringing glass-reinforced plastic to Ferrari bodywork

The Dino 308GT4 (left), launched in 1973, was nothing if not controversial, with a largely unloved body by Bertone and Ferrari's first ever roadgoing V8 engine. There has been very little criticism of the exquisite lines of the last of the big front engined V12 Ferrari's, the Daytona. The 1971 365GTS/4 Spider (above) and 1973 365GTB/4 coupé (below) are not only still among the world's fastest cars but certainly among the most beautiful

The Daytona was the last of the front-engined twelves and the Boxer was the first mid-engined. It took its name from the flat engine configuration shared by the contemporary GP cars and was put into production in 1973 as the 4.4-liter 365GT4 BB (or Berlinetta Boxer). This is a 1974 Spider version. The 1979 coupé (inset) has the 5-liter engine introduced in 1976 and the type number 512BB

All Forraris are thoroughbreds, tracing their blood-red heritage through wonderful racing cars like the 1958 world championship-winning Testa Rossa sports car (inset opposite), so called because of its red-painted cylinder heads. Today's range-topping car (main picture) bears the same name and has controls every bit as precise at those of old. The sumptuous but simple interior of the modern Testa Rossa is shown above

THE HISTORIC PRANCING HORSE

On 17 June 1923, Enzo Ferrari, driving a 3 liter works Alfa Romeo, won the first Circuit of Savio race, held near Ravenna. Ferrari won the race very convincingly against surprisingly good opposition and he also set a new lap record. It was one of the most impressive of about a dozen race wins in his career. Although, like most of the others, it came in a relatively minor event, this particular victory has a very special place in Ferrari history.

Among those who congratulated Ferrari was a local nobleman, Count Enrico Baracca. The Count was the father of Francesco Baracca, Italy's top-scoring fighter

pilot of the First World War, and he wanted to invite Ferrari to his home.

Francesco Baracca was born on his family estate near

Ferrari is proud of his name and proud of the Prancing Horse badge of the Scuderia Ferrari. The engine and cockpit of the marque's first World Champion, the 1952 500 (below), show both, and the road car (right) shows the badge at its best, on Italian racing red. Ferrari has never forsaken his national racing color and never will.

Ravenna in 1888 and in 1907, against his family's wishes, he enroled in the military academy in Ferrari's home town of Modena. From there, in 1909, he went to join the cavalry, but in 1912 he traveled to France to train as a pilot, qualifying within a few weeks and becoming an expert flyer and instructor.

Death of an air ace

When Italy entered the war in 1915 Baracca began a military flying career. He shot down his first victim in April 1916 and, having survived being hit and even forced down himself, he took his tally to 34 kills by mid-1918. Then on 19 June, flying a SPAD fighter along the Austrian front, he met his end. He was killed by a single bullet, probably from the ground, through his head. He crashed behind the enemy lines.

For his successes against the enemy, Baracca had received many awards, including Italy's highest award for bravery, the Gold Medal for Military Valor. In November 1916 he was also dubbed a Knight of the Air and, no doubt recalling his days in the cavalry, he added a crest to the side of his aircraft – a black prancing horse, the *Cavallino Rampante*, on a white background.

After Baracca's death, the emblem was apparently cut from his crashed aircraft and returned to his parents. That was how Ferrari came to be invited to the Baracca home.

There he met Francesco's mother, the Countess Paolina Baracca, and she dedicated her son's black prancing horse symbol to Enzo Ferrari, to bring luck to his racing cars.

Perhaps the Baraccas chose Ferrari of all racing drivers because of Francesco's connections, however sad, with Ferrari's native Modena; or perhaps, it has been suggested, because Ferrari's brother, Alfredo, had died during the war while in service with Baracca's squadron.

Honoring a legend

Whatever the true reason for the dedication, Ferrari regarded it as an honor and he gave it great dignity through his own unfailingly honest effort. He put the black prancing horse emblem onto a yellow shield, representing the civic color of Modena, and from then on every Scuderia Ferrari racing car and every road car except some of the Dinos has borne the famous badge. The sad tribute to Italy's lost flying hero is now one of the best-known motoring emblems in the world.

Ferrari's drivers are never allowed a moment's doubt about their allegiances; not only the steering wheel but every instrument on the 500's dashboard carries the Prancing Horse

Below: *A twelve cylinder E type with soft top retracted*

Next page: *US specification 1969 E type 2 plus 2*

JAGUAR

CHRIS HARVEY

Contents

SOAR-AWAY SUCCESS

The 70 years of success that surround Jaguar cars have been dominated by one name, that of Sir William Lyons (1901–85), knighted for his services to industry in 1956. He was, and remains, the inspiration behind every one of the stunning machines produced by this legendary British car manufacturer; the vision of this master stylist is still reflected in today's XJ saloons and XJ-S coupés.

Lyons, however, was not just a designer. He was an exceptionally talented businessman, who built up his company from small beginnings in a garden

shed in the northern English seaside resort of Blackpool, famous for its tourist attractions, among them its famous tower that resembles the Tour Eiffe in Paris.

The shed in question was used by William Walmsley, a coal merchant's son, to build sidecars for motorcycles. Walmsley was soon joined by another young man: his close neighbour, Lyons.

Lyons was only 20 years old when the pair went into serious production in 1922 as the Swallow Sidecar Company. But so great was the force of his

William Lyons was the man who made Jaguar. He is remembered generally as one of the most gifted stylists, but he was far more than that. Lyons, knighted in 1956, was one of the first real car designers, because he was responsible for the entire concept, even that of the engine. His talents extended further than that: an exceptionally able businessman, his foresight took Jaguar from a back street enterprise to a high-performance pinnacle.

Jaguar's sports models soon developed a reputation for extreme performance, but the mainstay of production was always the more mundane passenger cars. In the early days, because of their construction on a separate chassis, convertible editions of the basic saloons were relatively easy to build. This is a small 1.5-liter drophead.

One of Lyons's most spectacular early cars was the SS 100 sports model, which was one of the first to bear the name Jaguar. It was also the machine that created Jaguar's high-performance image — after a series of cars that looked faster than they were.

The more exotic Jaguars, such as this 3.5-liter drophead, featured some of the most exciting styling seen in the immediate postwar era.

Jaguar's reputation was swiftly reinforced by the D type sports racing car that made Le Mans its own. Its design by aerodynamicist Malcolm Sayer, closely followed trands established by contemporary aircraft. This example races on at Donington during 1989 in the hands of British driver Chris Drake.

The first car to gain massive publicity for Jaguar was the XK120. Its performance, price and appearance put it in a different league to any other sports car of the 1940s and early 1950s. This is the famous 1951 ex-works Alpine Rally car returning to its natural habitat on Italy's Passo Giau, in the hands of Mike and Gina Barker during the 1988 Classic Marathon.

personality and vision that the company soon expanded into making special bodies for cars such as the cheap new Austin Seven (on which BMW based its first product) and this sounded the death knell for the sidecars.

The move to Coventry

For a number of reasons, including the very success of this new enterprise, Swallow had to move from the north of England in 1928 to the Midlands, the heart of Britain's motor industry. Soon the firm was producing more and more parts for its cars, which now bore the new company name of SS, rather than just special bodies for other makers' chassis. Among the most spectacular SS products was a new range called Jaguar.

When the Second World War broke out in 1939, production was switched to aircraft components. With the return of peace in 1945, Lyons changed the name of his company from SS to Jaguar, because of the association these other initials had acquired.

A great new engine

The war years had not been wasted. Senior management performed their night-time firewatching duties in their offices... and occupied themselves with designing a new engine. This was entirely Lyons's concept, a production version of the twin overhead camshaft units that had powered pre-war racing cars. Experts said it was impractical to put such machinery into large-scale production, but Lyons stood his ground, and the famous XK engine appeared in a new sports car in 1948.

The speed and beauty of this car, the XK120, was sensational, but its price was even more exceptional. It was cheap because Lyons gambled on selling timeless products that would not need constant, and expensive, development. Soon the XK120 was joined by the Mark VII saloon, driven by the same engine. So much smooth power had been harnessed that Jaguars were successful in the world's top races and rallies. Only Ferrari and Mercedes produced cars that could match racing versions of the XK, called the C type and D type.

Ultimately, the production sports car developed into the XK150S, finished in all manner of extraordinary colours aimed at the booming North American market.

Amazingly, Jaguar had trouble selling surplus stocks of D type racers in the late 1950s, so converted some to a roadgoing specification and called them the XK-SS. This example is chassis XKD540, which retained its racer's XK engine

The big saloons (right), which made all the money for Jaguar, developed along similar lines to the sports cars, although they tended to more sober paintwork. This is the ultimate expression of the line pioneered by the Mark VII: the Mark IX of 1959.

Export success

Ferraris cost a fortune and were made only in very small numbers, so they posed no threat to Jaguar in the marketplace. Mercedes sports cars occupied a similar niche, although that company's reputation was enhanced by competition successes. However, Jaguars were cheap and exports boomed as they won the Le Mans 24-hour race five times, and the Monte Carlo Rally.

It was at the peak of this success, in 1955, that Lyons played another winning card. He introduced a new medium-sized saloon, the Mark 1, to fit neatly in his range between the sports cars and big saloons developed from the Mark VII.

In his biggest market, the United States, fuel was exceptionally cheap at that time. Small cars cost as much to develop as big ones, but people were ready to pay more for larger editions, and Americans liked enormous automobiles. Lyons therefore planned a really big saloon. Huge American V8 engines were beginning to match the power and torque of his smaller, more sophisticated XK unit. He wanted to stay one step ahead of the opposition, so design work began on a V12 engine.

In the meantime, in 1961, Lyons again swept the market with a production version of the D type racing car, the E type sports model, closely followed by his new saloon, the Mark 10, which he hoped would soon be powered by the V12. Medium saloons reached the peak of their development in the Mark 2.

Overleaf:
Jaguar sales reached fever point in the early 1960s with the E type production car, based on the D type sports racer. Like the XK sports cars before it, the E type was produced in 1964 in both open roadster and fixed-head coupé form.

Amalgamation and takeover

Lyons felt vulnerable in only one area. Jaguar was not sufficiently large to produce its own body panels, so he led his company into amalgamation with much of the rest of the native car industry in 1967 to form the British Motor corporation. This heralded the most successful Jaguar yet, the XJ6, a medium-sized development of the Mark 10, that would eventually be recognized as the Best Car in the World after it had received the V12 engine in 1972.

By then Britain's motor industry was in decline, but Jaguar's fortunes were revived for a while as a brilliant new leader, John Egan, took over in 1980.

Lyons lusted after even bigger profits from ever-larger cars, but went over the top with the enormous six-seater Mark 10. It proved too big to be a runaway success in Europe and established only a niche market in North America, where there was a surplus of large saloons that would soon be cut down to size by soaring fuel prices.

Problems with the Mark 10 mattered little to Jaguar for the company had brought out another winner, the medium-sized Mark 2 saloon, which became a top seller everywhere during the 1960s. This is the slim-bumpered 340 variant produced towards the end of the run.

The XJ6, which was developed from the Mark 10, featured the slimmer lines of the Mark 2 saloon and took Jaguar back to the top. Ultimately, it would be recognized as The Best Car in the World when it received a long-awaited V12 engine, which Lyons had hoped could be used in the Mark 10.

Eventually the 12-cylinder Jaguar engine (right) was adopted as an option across the range; it filled any underbonnet space, such as that in the XJ-S coupé, to capacity.

The company made considerable profits before a worldwide recession caused enormous problems for quality car makers, including Jaguar's rivals, Mercedes and BMW. Eventually the American giant, Ford, took over and Egan bowed out in 1990 as special Jaguar racing cars swapped world sports car championships with Mercedes. By then, so much had been invested in the name Jaguar that it took as if it would live on for ever.

Such, in brief outline, is the Jaguar story. Its main themes must now be looked at in more detail.

Gradually the North American market played a dominant role in the design of the Jaguar saloons. This Mark 2 version had been facelifted, with a raised bumper line and interior changes to meet ever more stringent safety regulations.

The XK engine became one of the longest-running in the British motor industry, but eventually a lighter unit had to be phased in. The new 3.6-liter unit made its début in the XJ-S before being adopted for the saloon car range.

Jaguar experimented with more austere, and economical to produce, interiors in its sporting models, but had to return to traditional leather and walnut in the late-model XJ-S to maintain its appeal.

Jaguar moved into the 1990s with a completely revised XJ6, while retaining the earlier bodyshell for the 12-cylinder unit. This was because the new engine bay had been designed only to take an in-line six-cylinder engine — during a battle for survival under British Leyland management, which wanted to instal a Rover V8!

SS FOR
SUPER SWALLOW

Swallow bodies were in a class of their own because William Walmsley was an exceptionally good stylist, and William Lyons learned much of the craft from him. More importantly, however, Lyons was also exceptionally good at running the business. He realized that their company must expand to survive and relied on his own ability to handle the growing pains. Walmsley was more cautious, preferring not to gamble.

However, even Walmsley could see that the days of making a living from selling good-looking — but expensive — sidecars were numbered, as cars like the Austin Seven offered more comfort, capacity, performance and safety at roughly the same price. At first he went along with Lyons's decision to make special bodies on the Austin Seven chassis because he liked producing beautiful things. They cost more to make but, it was hoped, Swallow could sell more.

Soon they expanded into building special Swallow bodywork on the Austin Seven chassis as the small British car swamped a market that had once been dominated by sidecars.

It was during this period that economic depression swept the world, but Swallow survived because many owners of large cars were forced to 'trade down' as times became harder. They did not want to be seen driving around in Austin Sevens, so they bought top-of-the-range Swallow-bodied versions!

Economic migration

By 1928 the cost of transporting chassis complete with mechanical running gear from the Austin factory in Longbridge, Birmingham, to Blackpool wiped out any savings Lyons could make by building bodies in Blackpool. The only possible alternative chassis were made by Standard, in Coventry, or Morris, further south in Oxford. In addition the need for Swallow to migrate was made imperative by sheer lack of space in Blackpool.

William Lyons and his partner, William Walmsley, launched their business from the back streets of the Lancashire seaside resort of Blackpool, producing adventurous bodies for motorcycle sidecars.

Nobody, other than Lyons, knew what the initials SS indicated: was it Standard Special, or Super Swallow, Standard Swallow or Swallow Special, or any other combination that used the same words? Lyons never revealed the secret.

The long, low SS saloon looked very fas[t] and sold well at a very low price for suc[h] a speciality.

The early SS engines were provided by the Standard Motor Co. of Coventry, leaving Lyons planning to produce his own.

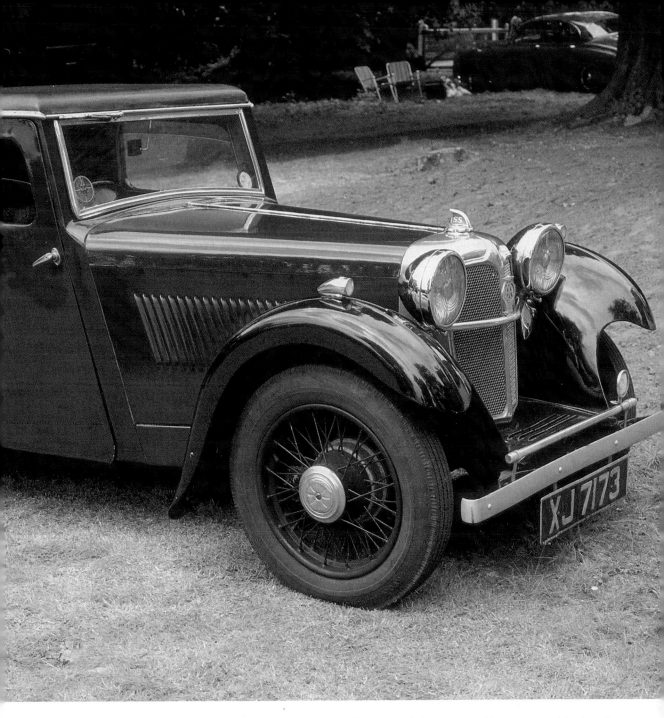

Industrial wages were higher in the Midlands, but skilled labour was more readily available and there were vacant premises, of a size that the growing Swallow enterprise needed. Soon the company was installed in a First World War ammunition factory at Foleshill, Coventry. Car bodies were the mainstay of production, on a range of chassis that was expanded to include the Italian Fiat, and the British Swift, Wolseley and Standard. Variations took in sporting two-seaters and luxurious little coupés, as well as saloons and a dwindling number of sidecars.

The first SS cars

By 1931 Swallow could be classed as a car manufacturer, rather than just a coachbuilder, for Standard was producing sufficient parts solely for the SS1 coupé. Lyons would never reveal what the initials SS meant — Standard-Swallow, Swallow-Standard, Standard Special or Swallow Special — and he took the secret to his grave.

The long, low, incredibly stylish SS1 not only looked fast, but represented an outstanding bargain at just over £300. Lyons's gamble in keeping down the price was justified by spectacular sales. Critics, however, alleged that the car was not as fast as it looked, so soon ever more powerful six-cylinder engines were fitted. Then in 1934 a smaller SS2 saloon was introduced to satisfy less flamboyant customers. By now, Walmsley felt that he had lost all control of the company he had helped create and resigned, devoting the rest of his career to producing caravans in a small way.

AAR 451

A new name: Jaguar

One of Lyons's first moves now that he had full
charge was to crate his own engineering
department, so that SS could continue to expand
and improve the performance of its cars without
others sharing its secrets. He hired a brilliant young
engineer from the Humber company, William
Heynes, and engaged the freelance Harry Weslake
to extract more power from the Standard engine.
His work was exceptionally successful and provided
enough power for a two-seater sports version of the
SS1 to reach 145 km/h (90 mph) and be called the
SS90. Further development reached a climax in the
3.5-liter SS100, which could reach 160 km/h — the
magic 100 mph for the British.

These glamorous new cars were called Jaguars
after the lithe South American hunting cat. Teething
troubles were so great that for a time Walmsley's
earlier anxiety over the pace at which SS was
expanding seemed as though it might be justified.

156

At first the Jaguar name was combined with the initials SS.

The new Jaguar line was endowed with a glamorous image by a stripped-down SS100 (below right), used on the Brooklands racetrack and called Old Number Seven after its chassis number.

One of Lyons's most adventurous moves was to switch production to all-steel bodywork. The investment nearly bankrupted his emergent firm, but immense efforts by the workforce saved the company and put it on course to become a major manufacturer. This is one of the first all-steel saloons, made in 1938.

The company nearly went bankrupt as Lyons had to borrow heavily in order to invest in the all-steel bodywork needed to meet an immense demand for the cars, a demand that could not be satisfied by the traditional wooden-frame methods of small-scale production.

Dedicated efforts by the new skilled workforce, reinforced by the best from Blackpool, saved SS as new models expanded the range to include a drophead coupé, a larger-engined saloon and a smaller one to replace the SS2.

War and a new power unit

By 1938 the company was producing 5000 cars a year and Lyons was considering manufacturing his own engines and chassis rather than having them made specially by Standard. Former Bentley racing ace Wally Hassan was taken on as chief experimental engineer under Heynes, along with a new chief engine designer, Claude Baily.

Then in 1939 war broke out and production had to be switched to aircraft components. Lyons, however, was ever efficient; as we have seen, he talked Heynes, Hassan and Baily into helping him design a new engine during their all-night civil defence sessions. They did not mind. It was better to look into the future than to stare into the dark.

The name was changed to just Jaguar after the Second World War. The leaping Jaguar mascot replaced the SS badge.

Whether they were made entirely from steel, or based around a traditional wooden frame like this 1.5-liter drophead, the new Jaguars were exceptionally attractive.

THE JAGUAR POUNCES

The initials SS were quietly dropped after the Second World War because of their sinister Nazi connotations; Lyons now simply called his cars Jaguars. They had sold well abroad before the war, so he was able to obtain precious supplies of steel, reserved for major potential exporters as Britain fought to repay debts accumulated during the conflict. The world in general was starved of new cars — even the United States had had to switch almost entirely to war production in 1942. The priority, therefore, was to produce as many cars as possible rather than to devote precious time and materials to the immediate development of new designs.

Saloons were more profitable than sports cars, so the pre-war range was continued with the exception of the SS100. Development centred on a new independent front suspension system for the Mark V saloon and drophead coupé in 1948 as the XK engine was got ready for production.

The renowned XK power unit

Jaguar's engineers had at first expressed misgivings about such an engine. They pointed out that its tremendous power potential might be offset by noisy driving systems needed for the overhead cams; difficulties in manufacture, resulting in a higher cost; servicing problems; and lack of reliability. None of these factors was sufficiently critical in racing car applications, but they could spell disaster on the road.

Lyons was not convinced by his engineers' assessments and insisted that production went ahead, stipulating in addition that the engine had to look impressive. The result more than lived up to his expectations.

Postwar development centred at first on revised editions of the pre-war saloons, such as this 3.5-liter model, the Mark V. Apart from heavier bumpers to suit the North American export market, it featured a much-improved independent front suspension system.

As new car buyers began to demand something new, rather than revamped pre-war models, publicized achievements became important. There was a long waiting list of manufacturers for the giant presses needed to stamp out new saloon car bodies. The XK engine was therefore housed in a sports car using a shortened version of the new chassis, which held the road better because of its independent front suspension. This new car, called the XK120, was not intended for large-scale production, but rather as a test bed for the new engine and to reap as much publicity as possible. However, it demonstrated such an amazing performance from its introduction late in 1948, it looked so beautiful, and it cost so little, that demand far outstripped supply.

Few other cars could match the XK120's 193 km/h (120 mph) top speed, so it was soon winning

The XK120 sports car not only provided a glamorous image to help sell Jaguar saloons, but it proved uncommonly good in competition.

The XK (right) became an all-time classic, providing wonderful sport for Britons Roy and Margaret Hatfield in the Tyrol during the 1990 Classic Marathon.

races as well, running as high as third at Le Mans in 1950. Demand was so great that Jaguar had to tool up for all-steel production as the lure of winning top races led the company to increase the power output and provide an even more aerodynamic body on a C type (C for Competition) version, which used a lighter chassis and improved rear suspension.

The sports car range was soon supplemented by a fixed-head coupé. This XK120 (right) from Chile leads a Ford 'doctor's coupé' of the type driven by world champion Juan Manuel Fangio, in Mexico's Carrera Panamericana road race.

Swiss exotic car specialist Martin Hugi demonstrates the prowess of his Jaguar C type (below right) by holding one of its contemporary rivals, an Aston Martin DB3, at bay on the British Silverstone circuit.

The American Team Veale storm in their XK140 coupé into Zacatecas during the Carrera Panamericana.

Competition successes

The firm was rewarded with victory at Le Mans against cars such as the Ferrari V12, which cost four times as much as the Jaguar, a result repeated in 1953 when aircraft-style disc brakes complemented an even greater power output from the XK engine.

Fixed-head coupé and drophead versions of the standard XK120 followed in 1951 and 1953 before the model received minor modifications dictated by the massive American market, such as heavier bumpers, and much-improved rack-and-pinion steering. this was called the XK140, although its was no faster than its predecessor.

A revolutionary new body, shaped and built like the fuselage of an aircraft, but still powered by the XK engine, became the D type in 1954. Although the body shape received Lyons's approval, this was the first Jaguar that he did not design. Credit for the D type goes to the former Bristol Aircraft Company aerodynamicist Malcolm Sayer.

His slippery shape and the power of what would become the ultimate XK engine, the 3.8-liter, helped top drivers like world champion-to-be Mike Hawthorn to set such a scorching pace at Le Mans — reaching speeds up to 290 km/h (180 mph) — that it won three times in succession between 1955 and '57. Mercedes, using special engines that could not be put into general production, moved on to Grand Prix cars, while Jaguar scooped unequalled publicity because buyers everywhere could identify with such a power plant.

The E type

By 1957 the basic sports car had progressed to the
more luxurious XK150, with disc brakes, and engine
capacities raised to 3.8 liters. Sales soared again as
the E type was put into production in 1961, with its
steel body and new independent rear suspension,
and the option of either fixed-head coupé, or open
roadster bodywork.

Along with the cheap and cheerful Mini, this
bargain-priced sports car became a symbol of the
Swinging Sixties, a decade that set all manner of
fashionable trends. Its 240 km/h (150 mph) top
speed set the world alight and continued to do
wonders for the sales of Jaguar saloon cars!

Jaguars line up again at Le Mans, during a celebration of the marque's competition history before the 1973 edition of the 24-hour race.

Jaguar D types race on at Silverstone ... and at tracks all over the world.

Jaguar's fabulous D type sports racer (far left) was produced in several distinct series: this is one of the first works cars, built in 1954 and pictured at Le Mans.

Racing became a low-key operation as Jaguar's engineering efforts were concentrated on the new V12 power unit, which was tested in a mid-engined prototype called the XJ13. New saloon cars were needed as well, so the demand on development time was immense. In the end, Jaguar could not justify the effort that would have been needed to produce new bodies and chassis at a time when new tyre technology was running riot. So the XJ13 stayed in mothballs until such time as the E type's performance had been sapped by ever more stringent exhaust emission regulations in its biggest market, the United States.

Then, in a re-run of what had happened with the original XK120, the E type was revised to use the V12 engine in 1971. Performance was restored, although the detail design of this new car was dictated by American demands to such an extent that it was far softer, and less sporting, than the earlier machines.

By 1975, ever more draconian American safety regulations outlawed the E type, which had its petrol tank underneath the tail. Jaguar had to design a new sporting car, the XJ-S, with fuel carried in a less vulnerable position over its rear axle. At the time it looked as though influences then dominant in the American market would outlaw open cars as hazardous, so the XJ-S was visualized as a fixed-head coupé. Since them, there has never been enough money to produce another uncompromising Jaguar sports car.

Last and rarest of the XKs, a 150S roadster pictured with its immediate successor, a 3.8-liter E type.

Sports cars as they used to be: the cockpit of Jaguar D type chassis number XKD406 with the gearlever close to hand, the headlamp dip switch next to it, and the handbrake, rarely needed, over to the left.

The Jaguar sports car range grew wider and more luxurious, as can be seen in this picture of a 3.8-liter XK150.

Not only was the first E type a beautiful car (top), but it took the world by storm after proving capable of an extraordinary 214 km/h (133 mph).

Above: After five years American legislators got to grips with the E type; thus they forced the headlights to be exposed on this 4.2-liter example.

Left: Last of the racing E types, a lightweight, low-drag coupé.

Eventually the new V12 engine appeared in a revised version of the E type, called the Series Three. This car represented the end of an era ...

Although it did not race, the XJ13 prototype (below) served an invaluable purpose in providing a mobile test bed for the new 12-cylinder engine.

The racing E types were to be replaced by a mid-engined sports car called the XJ13 (bottom), but the development programme needed proved impossibly time-consuming.

GRACE, SPACE AND PACE

When the new saloon, the Mark VII, was finally launched in 1950, it caused as big a sensation as the XK120, and created an even bigger demand. An important factor was that it looked so good. There were fewer constraints in designing an open sports car that had to carry only two people. Inevitably in the 1950s it would have a long bonnet — or hood when it crossed the Atlantic — which helped make it look purposeful. The problem in carrying out a similar design operation on a big salon that had to accommodate six in comfort — if it was to compete in the contemporary American market — was one of bulk. Lyons managed to minimize this bulky look by using long, flowing lines for the wings.

Thanks to the power of the XK engine, which could propel two tons of car at more than 160 km/h (100 mph), grace, space and pace epitomized the Jaguar legend. The Mark VII was also marketed at a highly affordable price, because Lyons relied on selling it in large numbers and not changing the body style too often. The American market, softened by the XK120, was very receptive. And the sheer originality of Lyons's lines stood Jaguar in good stead. The appeal would last for more than a decade, at a time when American rivals had to spend fortunes changing their body shape every year to persuade customers that anything new must be an improvement.

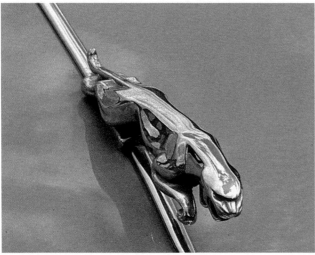

The leaping Jaguar mascot seemed to appear everywhere, especially on the saloons — but, oddly, never on the E types.

The Mark VII range (right above) soon progressed through the very similar Mark VIII to the ultimate Mark IX. This example still had the pace to provide Mario Marconi and Anthony Vorley with wonderful sport in the 1989 Classic Marathon on the Moistrocca hillclimb in Yugoslavia.

Jaguar's big new saloon soon made a name for itself in competition, thanks to the power that could be extracted from its XK engine.

Jaguar broke into a new market with the medium-sized Mark 1 saloon, a 3.4-liter example of which is seen holding its own in the Mexican Carrera Panamericana road race.

Thre were few faults with the Mark 1 Jaguar (below right), but they were all put right in the Mark 2. The 3.8-liter version was widely considered the ultimate saloon car transport.

Scottish father-and-son crew, Laurence and Gordon Grainger, conduct their fabulous 3.8-liter Mark 2 Jaguar through the Tyrol in the 1990 Classic Marathon.

Doughty contenders

The XK sports cars and the Mark VII saloon became the twin pillars of Jaguar's success in the early 1950s. As the XK became sleeker and fatter, the big saloons changed only in detail, offering automatic transmission from 1953 — initially to please the Americans and match Rolls-Royce and Bentley — and eventually, as we have seen, the 3.8-liter engine to keep abreast of the opposition.

Big as it was, the Mark VII, which progressed to similar Mark VIII and Mark IX models, proved itself no slouch on the racetrack, and dominated a new form of competition, for production cars, from 1953. Sales received another great boost when continuing success in the world's top rally, the Monte Carlo, was crowned with a win in 1956. Much of the Mark VII's success in this form of competition was attributed to an ability to plough through the most appalling snowdrifts in this wintery Alpine event.

The Mark 1 and Mark 2

In the meantime, Jaguar reinforced its range with a new medium-sized saloon, the Mark I, in which five people could be conveyed in great comfort. The big saloons used quite a lot of fuel, so for economy the first versions of this new car, produced in 1955, had an XK engine of only 2.4 liters. The performance hardly suffered, however, because Jaguar had invested much of the money made by the XK120 and Mark VII in producing a new bodyshell that dispensed with the need for a separate chassis. This unitary form of construction saved weight and resulted in a lower floorline; this in turn meant that the car slipped through the air more easily. The construction was stronger and stiffer than the earlier structure: softer suspension could be used as a result, improving comfort and handling.

This car represented the third big step forward for Jaguar, following the sensational body designs of

Lyons and the wonderful XK engine. Soon the Mark 1 was showing potential on the racetrack, and by 1957 Americans were demanding a bigger engine for even more performance. It was easy to drop in the 3.5-liter unit, which worked especially well with optional automatic transmission, but the price had to rise a little as well to pay for superior disc brakes.

Faults with the Mark 1, which went on to triumph on production car racetracks, were few. Most of them were eradicated in the Mark 2 version of 1959. This became the car beloved of businessmen and bank robbers alike, particularly when it acquired a 3.8-liter engine for ultimate performance. A wider rear axle improved handling, which had suffered a little because Lyons insisted that the Mark 1 should have rear wheel spats to make it look more elegant.

By then Jaguar's interior had set new standards of appeal for such a modestly-priced car. The retention of lots of leather and walnut, as in the products of Rolls-Royce, could only be justified by the larger quantities in which Jaguars were sold.

Acquisitions, amalgamation and upmarket luxury

As the Mark 2 saloon continued to dominate production car racing, and sales charts, it went further upmarket. By the 1960s Jaguar was beginning to outgrow its works in Coventry, yet no planning permission was forthcoming for expansion. Lyons therefore began buying up smaller manufacturers, including his near neighbours

The 3.8-liter Mark 2 (above left) appears to be the car for all seasons, as Geoff Maycock demonstrates during the Jaguar Drivers' Club challenge race at the Brands Hatch circuit in May 1989.

Battle of the heavy brigade (above), as Robert Buck (right), Mike Cann (centre) and Les Ely fight it out in 3.8-liter Mark 2 Jaguars at the Donington circuit in 1989.

The timeless lines of the Mark 2 saloon (right) are shown to good advantage as Andrew Ward rounds the hairpin at Cadwell Park in England during a Jaguar Drivers' Club race in 1989.

Daimler, and engine makers Coventry-Climax. The British Daimlers had been the cars of kings, and now their small 2.5-liter V8 engine was fitted to a more exclusive version of the Mark 2 saloon for the European market, badged as a Daimler. Acquiring Coventry-Climax provided not only additional engineering capacity, but returned Wally Hassan to the fold. He had moved across the road to Coventry-Climax earlier, and Lyons wanted him back to develop the V12 engine.

The great works achieved under William Heynes were many, not least a brilliant new independent rear suspension for the E type and Mark 10 saloon introduced in 1961. This unit was adapted in 1963 for yet another upmarket version of the Mark 2 saloon, called the S type.

As Jaguar phased in 4.2-liter editions of the XK engines in the 1964 E type and Mark 10, the range was further expanded by adopting the larger engine in a Jaguar 420 and Daimler Sovereign version of the S type from 1966. These were softer, even more luxurious cars, in keeping with the slower-revving engine. At the same time the original, by now rather heavy Mark 2 was slimmed down a little, in faster-revving 2.4-liter and 3.4-liter forms, as the 240 and 340 saloons. By 1968, with the amalgamation with the British Motor Corporation and the Leyland truck empire, to form British Leyland, now completed Jaguar was poised to introduce yet another world beater.

Jaguar Mark 2 saloons continue to prove popular mounts for European road tests. This 3.8-liter example of Richard Elvin and Colin Anderson is pictured near Reims during the 1990 Monte Carlo Challenge.

Champion Rob Newell charges on in the Jaguar Drivers' Club racing series with his Mark 2 saloon in 1986 (left below).

Jaguar saloons retained a classical British interior, dominated by walnut and leather, and this proved a great attraction at such an economical overall price.

Eventually slimmer bumper bars were adopted on the final versions of the Mark 2 saloon (below). This is a 2.4-liter 240 version built in 1968.

THE BEST CAR IN THE WORLD

The merger with the greater part of the British-owned motor industry to form British Leyland provided Jaguar with the backing to launch the new conglomerate's top model, the XJ6 saloon. Now that supplies of body panels were guaranteed through what had been the old Austin and Morris empire (makers of the Mini), Sir William Lyons felt that Jaguar could forge ahead.

His concern for the future had been heightened by the fact that he had no natural successor, his son having been killed in a car crash on the way to Le Mans in 1956. he had a gifted daughter but, sadly, the time for women to be accepted in Britain as top industrial decision makers had not yet come.

Lyons knew also that his successor's task would be formidable. For years he had kept Jaguar at the top of the sales charts by holding down the price of its products, frequently by cutting back on investment in production machinery. Inspired design, under his guidance, made up for a lot.

The Mark 10

Even a genius like Lyons could make mistakes. His greatest was the Mark 10 saloon. It was simply too big. By the time it went into production it was almost a relic of a bygone age. When it was conceived, the biggest profits were being made from the biggest cars, with the United States as the biggest market. To people who lived in a land with wide open spaces, long straight roads and vast resources, bulk was seen to be more of a virtue than a handicap.

Lyons could be forgiven in thinking that such people would not buy medium-sized cars in

Jaguar took the title of Best Car in the World from Rolls-Royce when it was able to insert the V12 engine in the chassis pioneered by the XJ6 saloon (below left).

The last Lyons-designed Jaguar was a pillarless coupé, seen in its ultimate XJ12 guise.

Many variants of the basic Jaguar range for the British and other European markets were badged as Daimlers, and had more luxurious fittings. This is a Sovereign Mark 2.

sufficient quantity to make his operation viable. It was not until it occurred to enough people that natural resources might run out that cars with a heavy fuel consumption became unfashionable. There was also the problem of road space. Europe began to run out of this before America, and roads were tighter anyway. Large, soft saloons therefore were never big sellers in this area. Eventually, parking space problems forced even the Americans to favour more compact cars.

The investment needed for a car as massive as the Mark 10, which was to replace the dated Mark IX, was almost impossibly heavy for a company still as small as Jaguar. The results had to be spread across the range. One of the prime needs was for a new form of rear suspension, good enough to cope with the immense power and torque generated by the XK engine (and even more from the projected

First of a new line in Jaguars, the XJ-S coupé, which replaced the E type sports car and lasted far longer than anybody expected — well into the 1990s.

Lyons's last engine (top left): the magnificent V12, created for the XJ12 and the XJ-S coupé that followed.

Eventually the XK engine had to be replaced, by the far lighter and easier to manufacture AJ6 (AJ for Advanced Jaguar) (above left).

TPH 330X

(V12). It also had to be cheap to produce and provide ride and roadholding far superior to what had gone before. That here Jaguar was able to produce simply the best in the world was the mainspring of their survival.

The Mark 10 that adopted this new independent rear suspension, and continued to use the XK engine, was really intended to take Lyons's last great gamble, the V12 engine that had defeated every other major car manufacturer who wanted to make money from big production runs. Sheer complexity was the main problem, smoothness of operation, power and torque the tantalizing objective.

Long, sweeping, separate wings were outdated by the time Lyons designed the Mark 10 in a gloriously old-fashioned session with the superintendent of his sawmills! The result was a

brilliant, all-enveloping car, fashioned like the spaceships prevalent in contemporary American films. Its only problem was that it was too big for the European market, so it had to rely on the more fickle tastes of the United States.

American advance and the Jaguar response

By 1961 America was developing new thin-wall casting techniques, which meant that it could produce immensely powerful traditional V8 engines relatively cheaply. Suddenly, top-of-the-range American saloons could keep up with a Mark 10 in the race away from the traffic lights. Sales of the model were good, but buyers preferred the Mark 2 saloon, which had no rival in the compact class, and the E type with no rival anywhere. However, with so

much money tied up in the Mark 10, the company could not easily switch its efforts.

The S type saloons, combining the appeal of the Mark 2 with the more advanced features of the Mark 10, were the first to move away. The 420 and the Daimler Sovereign, which was sold only in Europe, and the 4206 — just a Mark 10 in disguise — represented a holding operation. Something far better, combining the merits of them all, was on the way.

The XJ6

Lyons really got it right with his last great work, the XJ6. It combined all the attributes of the supremely luxurious 4206 in a bodyshell midway in size between the Mark 2 and the Mark 10. Dedicated development work, involving advanced radial-ply tyres, meant that it set new standards in the suppression of noise, vibration and harshness. These new tyres, a last fling by the British maker Dunlop, also endowed the XJ6 with fantastic new standards of ride and handling. As befits any car produced by Lyons, the appearance was exceptionally appealing, even if ever tougher, and conflicting, standards of international legislation led to compromises.

All the world rushed to buy this car in 4.2-liter, or European tax-busting 2.8-liter, forms. This was despite common knowledge that the XJ6 had really been designed for the V12 engine. Overcoming the problems of cooling such a bulky unit, which was stretched to an eventual 5.3 liters, was Hassan's last tremendous achievement. He stayed on past retirement age to see it into production with the E type of 1971, and shared his satisfaction with Lyons when the engine eventually found its way into the XJ bodyshell in 1972.

Hard-charging Scotsman Tom Walkinshaw put Jaguar back at the top on the racetrack, initially with XJ-S coupés — pictured winning at Donington in 1984 — painted in British Racing Green.

The national colour scheme was transferred to uncompromising sports-racing cars bearing the magic name Jaguar, pictured winning again at their home circuit, Brands Hatch.

Eventually Jaguar needed to take partners to win the world sports car racing chapionship, as can be seen from a livery dominated by Silk Cut, Castrol, and Dunlop.

The XJ12

This was an affluent year and Jaguar created a familiar sensation, demonstrating a five-seater saloon car that could outrun anything from Rolls-Royce or Mercedes at 235 km/h (145 mph), in greater comfort, with far better roadholding and at a much lower price. The only problem was that it used so much fuel, consumed at a rate as high as 23.54 liters per 100 km (12 mpg). By late 1973 the world had been hit by its first energy crisis and the XJ12, as this new saloon was called, looked like being an even bigger white elephant than the Mark 10. Again dedicated development helped. Fuel injection improved the consumption by as much as 50 per cent as British Leyland — struggling with all the problems of a major car maker in decline — starved Jaguar of funds and killed new projects, such as an improved transmission.

Last of the line: Jaguar's ultimate XK engine in 1978 XJ6 fuel-injection specification.

Few people have been able to make a Jaguar go faster — other than the Lister company, capitalizing on a famous backside name to promote customized versions of the XJ-S coupé (right) along lines pioneered by AMG for Mercedes.

Jaguar continues to produce the XJ-S V12 in ever more sophisticated editions: this is a 1989 version.

Saving Jaguar

As the E type died the XJ6, in 4.2-liter and economy 3.4-liter forms, was bringing in money. In 1975 Jaguar, with Lyons now an ageing figurehead, launched a coupé version of the XJ12, called the XJ-S. By now, Jaguar was left only with its engineering brains. The rest of the company, especially the production facilities, was worn out. Jaguar was dead on its feet when Michael Edwardes, a dynamic new head of British Leyland, brought in an engineer-turned-manager, John Egan, either to save the company or kill it at minimal loss.

Egan, later to become Sir John Egan for his services to industry, was very much of the free market persuasion. He tackled Jaguar's problems with such vigour that the marque's reputation was restored in the early 1980s. He instigated massive new investment and made millions through inspired financial control. He saved the XJ-S by using it as an exclusive test bed that sold well, like the XK120 before it. It was eventually available with first a Porsche-style Targa top, and then as a fully-open cabriolet that emulated the drophead XK150. It was during this period that the XK12 became recognized as the Best Car in the World because, quite simply, no other could match it.

A new range, an old rivalry

Under Egan's inspired leadership, Jaguar was able to launch a new range of XJ models, some in European Daimler guise, that would see the marque into the 1990s. There was, too a lighter new engine, the AJ6 (for Advanced Jaguar), which would evenutally lay the XJ to rest.

Then, as the ancient rival Mercedes realized it needed to seek a new performance image on the racetrack (an image more recently acquired by the local opposition in the form of BMW), Jaguar had to respond. What resulted were special racing cars that were the equal of the Mercedes machines, and used production-based engines for maximum publicity. The two great marques exchanged victories at Le Mans and in the World Sports Car Championship, until even Mercedes concluded it could afford no more, and dropped plans for the conflict to continue in Formula One.

By then, in 1991, Egan had left Jaguar, and the great British marque had been taken under the wing of the American Ford empire — with a product line that included the V12 engine and was strong as ever. Hopes remained of the massive investment in new models that Jaguar always needed.

The man who saved Jaguar, John Egan (right) with his 1990 fleet. From the left: a Daimler saloon, an XJ-S and an XJ6, with racing pedigree in the background.

Sweet and smooth: Jaguar's contemporary Sovereign saloon (below left).

Jaguar's XJ-S established a class of its own when it became available as a convertible. Nobody else made an open-topped V12 cylinder touring car, let alone one with such sophistication.

Below: *The eye-catching Jamara*

Next page: *The dymamic Islero S*

LAMBORGHINI

CHRIS HARVEY

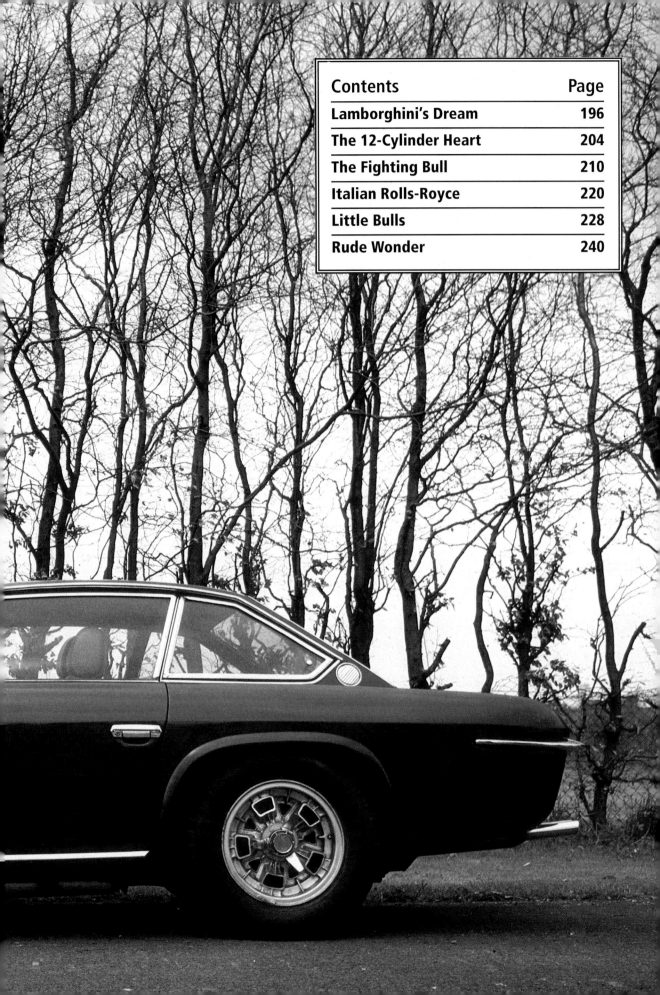

Contents

LAMBORGHINI'S DREAM

The name Lamborghini has become a symbol of the world's most exotic cars in some 30 years. This is because Lamborghinis are supremely Italian in character, the first one having been created in a typical explosion of passion. It was the result of the autocratic way in which the great manufacturer and racing team manager, Enzo Ferrari, treated both his customers and the people who worked for him.

One of his most ardent supporters had been the tractor magnate Ferruccio Lamborghini, a near neighbour in north-eastern Italy. When Lamborghini's new Ferrari proved troublesome, he asked for an explanation. None was offered, so he asked to speak to Enzo Ferrari personally. Ferrari refused to grant an audience to the self-made tycoon, so Lamborghini decided on the spot to build a better car with his own name on it.

At about this time, in 1961, six of Ferrari's top designers and technicians walked out, frustrated at his refusal to consider new ideas; small wonder, then, that they formed the nucleus that produced the marvellous new Lamborghini, seemingly overnight. The one who had the most influence was the consultant Giotto Bizzarrini, who had designed the chassis for the 250GTO, the most emotive Ferrari of all.

Ferrari had refused to let him use independent rear suspension, saying what had been good enough for generations of cars would serve him well. Bizzarrini was overjoyed to be able to demonstrate his talent with a new, all independently sprung spaceframe chassis for Lamborghini and a power unit as well.

In the early days, Ferruccio Lamborghini (above) was the dominant influence behind the creation of some of the world's greatest cars. Later he retired to cultivate wine. He is pictured at his own vineyard in 1990.

Ferruccio Lamborghini wanted nothing more than to see his name (left) on the best cars in the world.

Lamborghini's business empire was created around the manufacture of agricultural machinery. Tractors bearing his name are made by Fiat.

LAMBORGHINI 400 GT 2+2

Lamborghini's first car was the 350GT (above). This is the fifth one made, which he has confirmed is the oldest surviving Lamborghini. The first four examples were destroyed, although cars bearing the first chassis plates were built later by the Lamborghini factory.

Firms like Ferrari and Maserati had to take the new Lamborghini seriously — and increased the performance of their own cars. Lamborghini responded by enlarging the original 3.5-liter engine to 4 liters and giving the 400GT 2 + 2 two small rear seats (top).

The 350GT, the first Lamborghini

Lamborghini dictated its format. The number of cylinders was critical for fellow tycoons obsessed with prestige, glamour and status. He would have liked 16 cylinders, one stage better than the Ferrari opposition, which at that time had just 12. Eight was not enough because a new rival ironically enough designed by Bizzarrini for the Italian refrigerator concern Iso used an American V8 engine; six cylinders were for the middle class; four for the man in the street; and two were for the poor who could hardly afford to tax a car.

Sixteen cylinders would have made the engine too long, however, so Lamborghini settled for 12.

Lamborghini created a sensation by producing the mid-engined Miura in 1966, frequently painted in colours such as bright yellow and lime green.

But it had four overhead camshafts, rather than just two, so it was still better than a Ferrari.

Lamborghini had equally strong ideas about the body. It had to have a nose like a Jaguar E type, a tail like an Aston Martin DB4, with features from the Chevrolet Corvette and the Ferrari Superfast. Stylist Franco Scaglione did his best with this blend, but the new 350GT looked far from perfect when it was unveiled in 1963.

Meanwhile Lamborghini had hired a bright young design team headed by Giampaolo Dallara, Paolo Stanzani and a dour New Zealand racing mechanic called Bob Wallace. Although they were happy to improve the 350GT, and the 400GT that followed,

their main interest lay in showing the world what a wonderful racing car they could produce.

The beautiful Miura

Lamborghini left them to their dreams, then said: 'It means little to produce the best racing car in the world. People remember only the drivers. If you can produce the best road car in the world, nobody will ever forget it.'

As it happened, the mid-engined racing car that his bright young men wanted to make proved uncommonly good on the road. It needed only a brilliant new body, by Marcello Gandini, for the Miura to take the world by storm in 1966.

It was at that point that Ferruccio Lamborghini was at his most creative. Now that he had the best sports car in the world he wanted the best saloon, an Italian Rolls-Royce.

The Countach and the Urraco

In 1968 the resulting Espada became the world's fastest four-seater. That was not enough for Lamborghini. Development could not stand still and Stanzani and Gandini collaborated in 1971 to reveal an even more fantastic sports car, the Countach. It took three years to put this wedge-shaped wonder into production as Lamborghini tried to expand into Porsche's market: smaller sport cars produced in greater quantities.

By the time his 'mini-Miura', the V8-engined Urraco, appeared in 1973, the world's economy was in crisis. Car sales slumped, with those of high-performance machinery suffering the most. However, Lamborghini somehow survived, even though old Ferruccio, tired of such problems, retired to a vineyard to produce his own wine. Various managements battled on to produce updated Urracos, such as the Silhouette in 1976, and the Jalpa in 1982. The company even took a tilt at what was then a lucrative Middle Eastern market and built the world's most exotic jeep.

The backbone of production was always the Countach, however, in ever faster and smoother forms. The main problem was that the car was so complex that it had to be made by hand and there was not enough skilled labour to produce more than a handful. As the world economy came out of recession the Countach continued to sell well; and then in 1987 the American giant Chrysler, searching for prestige, bought Lamborghini.

The long, low Lamborghini Espada of 1968 became the worlds fastest car with four full-sized seats, and it has proved impossible to match.

Lamborghini pitched at a far wider market with the small and incredibly nimble Urraco (above right), aiming to topple Porsche from its throne. This is the Urraco in its ultimate 3-liter S form.

The Middle Eastern market spent massive sums of money on eye-catching cars in the 1970s. Lamborghini responded with the world's most strikingly different jeep to complement the Countach, which was so popular with Arabian sheikhs.

Lamborghini

lamborghini

Lamborghini

BO · B99858

The Diablo

By this time there were cars that could match the Countach for sheer exotic appeal. Chrysler therefore funded an operation to produce a new V12 supercar that would again put Lamborghini far ahead. Inevitably, there were clashes of personality and, rather in the manner of the Ferrari reorganization of 1961, many of the old team left to produce, at long last, a 16-cylinder car. This was the American-financed Cizeta. With a body designed by Gandini, it looked just like a new Lamborghini.

The car in this latter category was, however, the Diablo. The irony was that this too had a body designed by Gandini, but honed in a Chrysler wind tunnel to make it capable of a world-beating 328 km/h (204 mph). Meanwhile, consultants associated with Lamborghini produced Formula One GP engines; so after its first three decades Lamborghini was as vibrant as ever.

After this brief outline of the remarkable Lamborghini story the following pages will fill in more of the absorbing detail.

Lamborghini struggled for years to replace the Countach with something even more exotic, but had to wait until 1990 to create the 328 km/h (204 mph) Diablo .

The backbone of production from the Lamborghini factory at Sant'Agata Bolognese became the fabulous Countach, first seen in 1971 and pictured here leaving the production lines in its early form.

THE 12-CYLINDER HEART

Twelve cylinders have always been at the heart of the cars that made Lamborghini famous, and Giotto Bizzarrini's design was long-sighted. It also fitted in well with Lamborghini's ideals. Parts that could be changed around easily had always been one of the strengths of his tractor production. So similar principles were used in the V12 engine.

Bizzarrini used the same 77 mm (3.03 in) bore as Ferrari's top roadgoing unit, but made the stroke smaller so that the same power could be liberated by twin overhead camshafts on each bank of cylinders from a smaller overall capacity of 3.5 liters. This engine could then be uprated to 4 liters to give more power than the equivalent Ferrari of similar size, and even more with a larger capacity. The angle between the cylinder banks was kept down to 60 degrees, so that the overall width would not hamper chassis design.

Meanwhile Lamborghini designed a marble palace of a factory at Sant'Agata Bolognese, just 15 m (9 miles) from his tractor works at Cento, and 30 m (19 miles) from Ferrari at Maranello. Bizzarrini's old chief at Ferrari, Carlo Chiti, had left at the same time to join the ATS racing car project, which helped produce the engine.

As work progressed on the power unit, Bizzarrini designed the chassis. He produced two versions, one for competition and one for touring, as Lamborghini went away to decide what he really wanted: a competition car or a grand tourer. When he opted for a grand tourer, Bizzarrini left to build his own racing cars, but the influence of the legacy he left was far-reaching.

A young team

Dallara, brought in by Lamborghini at this stage, was a former pupil of Chiti. Although he was only 24

Although the name Bertone would forever be associated with Lamborghini coachwork, the first bodies were in fact buillt by the legendary Superleggera method — the hallmark of Touring of Milan (left above).

The original 3.5-liter engine filled the 350GT's underbonnet area to perfection (left below). There was nothing to match the impresssive sight of this 1963 unit with its six Weber carburettors, four overhead camshafts, and two banks of six cylinders.

This is the oldest Lamborghini in the world, and one of the rarest: the original two-seater 350GT, which has covered only 4582 km (2847 miles) from new. It is pictured on the estate of its anonymous owner, who has a fantastic collection of similar cars.

ears old, Dallara was a brilliant designer and produced an all independently sprung chassis that was similar to that of the Ferrari 250GTO, updated along Bizzarrini's lines. His assistants, Stanzani and Wallace from Ferrari's rival supercar makers, Maserati, run by Dallara's cousin Giulio Alfieri were only a year older.

At the same time Lamborghini told Dallara to design a new, smaller, V8 version of the V12 engine. This would use as many common parts as possible so that it could be produced on the same machinery. The idea was to enter the higher volume market for smaller sports cars at a later point and to be able to spread the eventual cost of buying expensive new machine tools.

The interior of the Lamborghini 350GT followed classic Italian lines, and was of far better quality than the Bertone products that followed. The lines of Bertone's bodies were priceless, but the attention to detail by Touring was matched only by British manufacturers like Jaguar. Rolls-Royce lacked sporting appeal, but put everybody else in the shade when it came to comfort.

When all the V12 development work was completed, with power reduced from 360 to 270 bhp for reliability, it was calculated that Lamborghini would be able to undercut Ferrari's price. So work went ahead and Bizzarrini commissioned his old friends, Neri and Bonaccini, who had produced the Ferrari 250GTO chassis, to make the Lamborghini frame.

In classically Italian manner, Lamborghini decided to go one better than Ferrari by having synchromesh on the reverse gear of his five-speed transmission, so that patrons could park more easily! Huge disc brakes all round ensured that they had no trouble stopping.

Body problems

Lamborghini was not so good at designing bodies, however, and sales were slow at first, even though the lines of his prototype had been much improved

The 400GT 2 + 2 followed the lines pioneered by the 350GT, but had a bench seat behind the two front bucket seats and featured the 4-liter engine.

One of Ferruccio Lamborghini's favourite cars was the Islero. He was responsible for its entire design, and drove one for years after it had become obsolete. When Lamborghini retired to grow grapes in northern Italy, there was only one thing missing from his life: an Islero. Finding one in good condition was hard, because so few were made. But British car dealer Barry Martina had the answer. When a customer, who had spent a huge sum restoring an Islero to immaculate condition, tired of his toy, Martina bought it — and presented it to Lamborghini so that it should always remain in his private collection.

by Touring, who had built it. This was partly because Italy was in the throes of one of its periodic financial crises, and partly because the 350GT had only two seats. The car's potential, however, was obvious and Dallara concentrated on squeezing in two small rear seats to widen its appeal. Steel panels replaced aluminium for economy and the weight went up. The capacity was increased to 4 liters in the 400GT 2 + 2 of 1966, producing 320 bhp to maintain its superiority over rivals from Ferrari, Maserati, Iso and Aston Martin.

One-off variants appeared with bodies by such firms as Zagato as Lamborghini wrestled with his styling problems. Top firms, such as Bertone, steered clear of a tycoon who tended to copy the ideas of others rather than allow the others to create an original. Nuccio Bertone told him: 'You are new to this game. You have a lovely car, but it is too much like a Ferrari. Let us wait until you have something really special. Then we will built you a body better than you have ever seen before, and together we will put Ferrari in the shade.'

Bertone could adopt this attitude because he had one of the best young designers in the business: Giorgetto Giugiaro. Nevertheless he had to look to the future. He knew that one day he would need Lamborghini because his main rival, Sergio Pininfarina, was enjoying an exclusive relationship with Ferrari.

The ailing coachbuilders, Touring, produced a wonderful two-seater open version of the 350GT, but could make only two of these GTS models because the 400GT was imminent. However, some two-seater 350GT cars were fitted with 4-liter engines to use up stockpiled parts, and these were given the 400GT designation. Touring even managed to make one 400GTs version before the firm expired through lack of work in 1967.

Less than original

As Maserati hit back with such beautiful cars as the Ghibli, Lamborghini collaborated with the former Touring designer Mario Marazzi to produce a new two-plus-two-coupé, the Islero. This was based on the 400GT 2 + 2, styled along similar lines to the Ghibli. Again, this was not an original and it failed to set the world alight. Maybe Lamborghini did not wish it to do so: 'I wanted a car that was not quite s exotic. Something more suitable for a businessmar who does not want to be dubbed a playboy.'

He was quite happy to adopt that attitude. Already Lamborghini had plans for a fantastic new saloon and all the world was raving over his new mid-engined sports car.

Ferruccio Lamborghini followed Jaguar practice when it came to designing the interior of his personal cars. So the Islero (top) had a wood-rimmed steering wheel, walnut facia, and the rocker switches of the late 1960s, whereas the earlier 350Gt had the machine-finished aluminium and toggle switchgear of the early E type sports car.

The graphics of early Lamborghini badges were symbolic (center): the darting S above the Islero script denotes a body built by survivors from the Superleggera era at Touring, led by designer Mario Marazzi, who worked in close collaboration with Ferruccio Lamborghini.

The influence of Maserati's timelesss Ghibli can be clearly seen from this contemporary picture of an Islero (right). The trouble was that the Ghibli came first, and the only people who could afford such exotic cars wanted an original.

THE FIGHTING BULL

Young men do not give up easily. Dallara still wanted to build a racing car and studied the most exciting one in existence, the mid-engined Ford GT40. Such a project would boost sales, he argued. Lamborghini listened, but did nothing. He had already decided privately that it was a waste of time and money to try to beat Ferrari at this game. Old Enzo was still winning world championships. His only problem was that his over-priced road cars let him down. Lamborghini, on the other hand, needed the young blood that was drawn by an urge for recognition in racing.

He therefore let Dallara, Stanzani and Wallace have their heads, allowing them to work in their spare time on a prototype mid-engined car in the mould of a Ford GT40. When they produced it for his approval, hoping that he would be so excited he would want to go racing, Lamborghini just sad: 'Sorry. Racing cars are not for me. But don't be upset. You have just created the most immortal road car. All we need is a body by Bertone. And Nuccio has promised this to me.'

Geneva Show sensation

The task of creating this immortal look fell to Bertone designer Giugiaro, who was just about to join the rivals Ghia. The work was therefore passed to his assistant, Gandini. He was another bright young blood anxious to prove himself at a time when Ferrari was stagnating, and Maserati and Aston Martin seemed to be stuck in a front-engined rut. His P400 Miura took the 1966 Geneva Show by storm.

The venue had been chosen because it was the early season meeting place of rich, sporting clients. The name meant as much. The P stood for Posteriore, denoting the then revolutionary idea of mounting the engine behind the driver, and Miura for the Spanish fighting bull: a more ferocious and formidable animal than Ferrari's prancing horse.

To Lamborghini's joy the orders flowed, despite a high price. He remarked: 'This means so much

Ferruccio Lamborghini recognized the need for original names for his cars. He favoured anything associated with bullfighting, where the bull was superior to the horse — the emblem sported for so long by Ferrari. Small wonder there is a statue of a fighting bull in the halls of Sant'Agata.

The heat generated by Lamborghini's 12-cylinder engine, mounted very close behind the seats, was immense. And rearward vision was distinctly restricted. Dallara solved this problem at the stroke of a pen with a double-glazed back window to insulate the driver and passenger, and a louvered engine lid to let out the heat and give a wide field of view to the rear-view mirror.

This is the Miura (far right), the car that established Lamborghini's reputation. It was designed almost by accident, in an attempt to persuade Ferruccio Lamborghini to go racing. He refused, and in 1966 released the most stunning road car on a world waiting with baited breath.

The long, flowing lines of the Miura put Bertone — and Gandini — on a pinnacle. In 1966 there was nothing in the world which looked like this Lamborghini or went anything near like as well. The Ford GT40 on which it was based was crude by comparison, and was rated only on the racetrack.

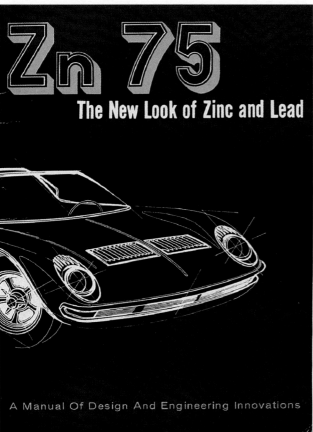

Zn 75

The New Look of Zinc and Lead

A Manual Of Design And Engineering Innovations

more than winning a race which everybody will forget within a few weeks. People will talk of this new car for years and remember that it has the same name as that on my tractors and the new central heating plant that I have just started.'

Miura refinements

The Miura needed a lot of refinement before it was ready for the road. One of the main problems was the noise and heat generated by the V12 engine mounted transversely only a few inches from the cabin. Such discomforts might be accepted by racing drivers, but not by well-heeled buyers. Wallace managed to minimize the problem with 1000 mm (39 in) of insulation, and a double-glazed rear window behind a slatted engine lid.

The Miura (top) was built like a racing car and offered its owners macho appeal. The front opened up like Jaguar's D type sports racing car, and the back demonstrated the same thinking, because that was where the engine was.

Subsequently, the open Miura was sold to the International Lead Zinc Research Organization for research and was featured in a brochure advertising the latter's wares.

The windscreen of the open Miura was re-angled with a small top rail, and the engine compartment line was lowered. Because of windscreen stressing problems, however, the car was not intended for production, but merely to attract custom for coachbuilders Bertone.

The chassis was influenced by a parallel helicopter project in which Dallara had been engaged by Lamborghini. It had a central pod for the occupants with all-independent suspension ung front and back. The engine was the same

internally as the 400GT but used a different main casting, which included the transmission casing. Stanzani helped reduce high-pitched whining by reversing its normal rotation!

The nose was kept exceptionally slim for the most efficient air penetration, which meant that the lighting was inadequate for anything like a maximum speed of around 275 km/h (170 mph). Lamborghini laughed off criticism by joking about how prospective clients ought to spend their nights.

Aircraft practice was also well illustrated in this exceptionally low car by the way the main switches occupied a cluster in the roof above the driver.

Demand was his for any Miura, so work
on special editions was slow. Eventually,
Bertone built an open version to show at
Brussels in January 1968.

Colour schemes tended to be garish, in the manner of the late 1960s, with lime green as one of the most popular hues. Miura owners also started a trend by having normally brightly plated fitting painted matt black, to emphasize the macho image.

No racing

Soon Dallara tired of trying to persuade Lamborghini to go racing and left for the emergent Italian rival firm of De Tomaso. Stanzani took over with another young engineer, Massimo Parenti, to assist him. As they worked on new models, Wallace concentrated on development, ironing out bugs that became apparent in the Miura. His initial efforts resulted in an increase in the standard power output to 370 bhp for the 280 km/h (175 mph) Miura S; the same basic engine appeared in the Islero S. Many Miuras were also fitted with a front spoiler to reduce nose lift.

Wallace and Stanzani still hoped to go racing so they built a lightweight Miura, called the Jota, or Iota, because they thought it had power of an atomic order. Problems with the engine sharing the same oil supply as the transmission were eliminated on the Jota by the use of separate castings. Wider wheels and more modern tyres were also fitted.

Many of the lessons learned on the Jota were carried over to a new model, the Miura SV (for Super Veloce: 'extra fast'), launched at the 1971 Geneva Show. At first it was built only to special order, until existing stocks of Miura parts were exhausted. Then its engine, in 385 bhp tune and with separate castings, became a standard fitting.

In this form the Miura stayed in production until 1975; and several replicas of the Jota were built for favoured customers.

Expense was not a primary concern when the open Miura (above) was rebuilt with as many metals, alloys, coating and plating processes as possible that came under the umbrella of its new owners. It was therefore given a proper leather interior to show that they were not prejudiced entirely in favour of lead and zinc!

Lamborghini 4-liter engines (right), even with the standard side-breathing carburettors, were so efficient that they found themselves in the forefront of international power boat racing — not least because Ferruccio Lamborghini had a high-speed yacht he was especially proud of.

The Miura (far right) was able to use more efficient vertical Wever carburettors than the horizontal units in earlier cars because its engine lid followed a higher line — although it had been lowered as far as possible in the Lead Zinc Research car dubbed the Zn 75.

Some of the castings featured on the open Miura were fantastic. People who saw it on show all over the world in the late 1960s had never realized it was possible to create such perfect forms as those of a Lamborghini air intake in lead or zinc (top).

The gearlever (above) on the open Miura was one of the few controls that an aspiring owner could touch with open hand — which meant that it had to be an art form, in lead, zinc, or whatever.

ITALIAN ROLLS-ROYCE?

Lamborghini found that he had five times as many customers as he had expected for the Miura, so he promptly forgot about it and concentrated on what he anticipated would be his next blockbuster, a full four-passenger saloon using similar mechanical components. He insisted that it should be long and low, not 'upright and stodgy' like the British Rolls-Royce it would meet head-on in a high-priced marketplace.

The Marzal unveiled

Marcello Gandini, fired by the success of the Miura, approached his brief with wild enthusiasm. His early ideas were concentrated on developing an in-line, six-cylinder, rear-engined, rather than mid-engined, version of the Miura, stretched to accommodate four seats. Access was all important and he decided the easiest way to get in and out of what would be a very low car was through gullwing doors. He emphasized that four full-sized seats were provided by making the doors almost entirely from glass. With so much glazing, air conditioning was essential and so it became part of the design, along with futuristic hexagon formations.

When this car, dubbed the Marzal after another fighting bull, was unveiled at Geneva in 1967, the

Ferruccio Lamborghini was concerned. The car he wanted to topple Rolls-Royce from its 'Best Car in the World' pinnacle should present a totally different image from the comtemporary British products. Back in the Edwardian era, Rolls-Royce cars were quite fast. That aura had been maintained during the 1930s by buying the rival Bentley company, so that there was an alternative for customers who craved the quality of comfort a Rolls-Royce offered, but were worried that the offering was too heavy. Lamborghini's new car had to be faster than anything else in the world that offered leg room comparable to a Rolls-Royce; yet at the same time it had to have the same sort of dignity. The result was probably one of the greatest, and most underrated, Lamborghinis: the Espada achieved all those objects and failed only in that its makers did not have the money to develop the concept fully.

The seating plan (below) in an Espada was of paramount importance. Once it could be demonstrated that you could sit in comfort in the back, and travel at the same speed — or quicker — than any rival, sales were limited only by how many Lamborghini could make.

overall effect was just as stunning as that of the Miura had been. Lamborghini loved the publicity but vowed never to make another, because it looked too much like a spaceship. His chief objection was to the very basis of the design, the gullwing doors: 'What kind of man', he asked, 'wants to sit in a car, showing his lady's legs to all the world?' He also remembered how, 10 years earlier, Mercedes had had to abandon their glorious Gullwing coupé because of American objections that occupants would be unable to get out of such a car if it overturned.

In concept the Espada (above) was very much like the Miura, as can be seen from this all-action photograph. This classic design was a tribute to the talents of Lamborghini, Gandini and Wallace.

The interior of the Espada, which was derivative in so far that it aped that of the contemporary Jaguar saloons in its use of walnut and black velour.

When viewed in planform (above right), it is possible to see why the Espada was such a brilliant machine. It slipped through the air with all the grace of a big sports car.

The low-slung Espada

o the Marzal remained a show car and the Bertone
ompany was told to produce something else
uickly if it wanted to carry on building Lamborghini
odies. Happily, the firm had just completed another
how car, the Pirana, based on the front-engined
aguar E type. It was an easy decision to combine
lements of the Marzal with this show car,
specially as Lamborghini liked it.

The fact had to be faced, however, that this car
ould be a good deal heavier than the Marzal, and
e front location of its engine was an essential part
f the design. Therefore a chassis was constructed
at amounted to a front-engined Miura equipped
ith the running gear from the Islero. Elements of
e Marzal's advanced styling were retained,
though it now had a conventional door each side,
o wide that access to the rear seats was easy. The
ew car, called the Espada after the sword that

killed fighting bulls, was even lower than the Islero,
so it could hardly be called upright and stodgy.

Maximum speed touched a magic 240 km/h (150
mph), so the Espada created at the 1968 Geneva
Show what was becoming a traditional Lamborghini
sensation. The power unit was later uprated to
Islero S specification, although the Espada did not
receive this designation because Lamborghini still
felt that it should be regarded as a calm, dignified
saloon car rather than something wild and exciting.

Difficulties with the Jarama

By 1970 the Islero was looking decidedly dated,
while the success of the Espada as the world's
fastest four-seater saloon continued unabated.
Lamborghini therefore followed an obvious route by
producing a short-chassis coupé with two small rear
seats as the Islero's replacement. This was given
the name Jarama, after an area in Spain famed as

much for its fighting bulls as its racetrack. The bodywork, again by Bertone, was stunning, especially as it now featured flared wheel arches that made the car look even wider and more purposeful.

This became the first Lamborghini to miss its mark, however, because of intense competition from Maserati with its classic Ghibli, and Ferrari with the Daytona, which was to become that company's greatest front-engined road car (as opposed to a road racer like the GTO).

Wallace had his work cut out to ensure that the Jarama maintained the Espada's superb reputation for handling as he worked on new models, and fought against time to perfect the Miura in its final form as the SV. Such as the competition from Ferrari, Maserati, and Aston Martin with a new V8, that Lamborghini had to stick to cheaper steel panels. As a result the bulky Jarama weighed in at 698 kg (1540 lb) against the Islero's 596 kg (1315 lb), and there was not sufficient time to pare off the extra pounds by intensive development of the

Bertone had every reason to be proud of the Espada, and emphasized this with a symbolic B above his nameplate (top left).

The name Espada (center) was a reference to the sword that killed the fighting bull. As such, it represented a further assertion of superiority to Ferrari's prancing horse. Immortal Italian graphics on the flanks of the Espada emphasized the principle.

Under-bonnet room (left) was at a premium in the Espada, so much so that the Series One cars relied on a steering box rather than the more precise rack-and-pinion. Problems presented themselves when the steering box tore itself out of its mountings while the car was being parked. It was left to Wallace to solved this dilemma by adopting a power-assisted system, developed by the German firm ZF, for the Series Three Espada of 1973.

Wallace, along with Gandini and the Lamborghini management, made sure that the Jarama looked the part of a futuristic 2 + 2 seater about to take over from the Islero and combat the best from Ferrari, Maserati and anybody else who could survive in the financially restrained 1970s. As it happened, there was not enough development capacity (nor, more to the point, money) to pare down the Jarama's weight which would have made it so much better than an Espada.

floorpan. This meant that although it was still capable of 261 km/h (162 mph), it did not enjoy the massive advantage in performance over its rivals that Lamborghini customers had come to expect.

Efforts were then concentrated on making the Jarama more luxurious and on giving it extra power in an S variant available from 1972. Soon after this both the Espada and the Jarama were listed with automatic transmission aimed mainly at the North American market. The unit fitted came from Chrysler because this was considered the best.

It was during 1973, when the first automatic Espadas and Jaramas were being sold, that Stanzani gave up trying to think of anything to replace the Espada. There was no evident way of conveying four people more quickly in even greater comfort: a fact of life that has received tacit consent from German supercar makers who today agree to limit the top speed of their cars to 250 km/h (155 mph).

And so the Espada and Jarama continued with minor revisions until 1978, when continuing world financial crisis forced this great Italian manufacturer to concentrate on the sports cars that made the most money.

Lamborghini engines always look glamorous, even when installed in the relatively modest base of a Jarama.

Lamborghinis are dream cars. Paint the bonnet black, open it up to expose the engine to all the world, and you really feel that you have a world beater.

LITTLE BULLS

Nobody could tell Ferruccio Lamborghini what to do. He could cruise whenever he wanted to in his yacht, powered by two Lamborghini V12 engines. He could drive around wherever he wanted to go in his Islero, the car he designed himself; or his tiny Fiat 500, favoured by the poor working folk of northern Italy, who would always be his brothers and sisters. Small wonder, again, that he told Stanzani: 'Make me a little Lamborghini. The Marzal has grown too big. Maybe it is still possible to build a small sports car. The Porsche 911 is about the right size.'

The Urraco: a rival for Porsche

Paolo Stanzani's only problem was that such a small, nimble car would have to have two small rear seats to be competitive with the 911. Already Ferrari was discovering this with the Dino, which had only two seats. That made Lamborghini even more determined to have a 2 + 2.

The chief trouble with the Porsche, in Stanzani's opinion, was that the engine was in the wrong place. The space for rear seats had been liberated only by placing the power unit behind the rear axle, which caused handling problems. With the help of Marcello Gandini, Stanzani managed to find room for both an engine and seats within a sufficiently short wheelbase by angling a V8 so that one bank of cylinders occupied the space above its transverse transmission.

A capacity of 2.5 litres was chosen so that power could be readily uprated in the manner of the V12. A

Lamborghini thought that salvation had been found with the Urraco (right), the 'little bull' that could outhandle the notoriously nervous Porsche 911.

By the time Lamborghini had perfected the Urraco in its 3-liter form, it was too late. Porsche had produced the ultimate wild animal, a Carrera RS. This was so savage, and at the same time so practical, that it made a mockery of the Urraco's far superior handling.

Lamborghini never forgot its heritage. Even as pictures were being taken of the contemporary Jalpa, there was a Miura lurking in the background.

Changing tyre technology had more effect on Lamborghini than almost any other car manufacturer in the mid-1970s. With immense support from Pirelli, the firm pioneered the low-profile tyres that have changed the face of motoring. Sadly, there were no sponsors who would pick up the sort of money that Gandini would have needed to change the face of a Countach — or Urraco — to conceal such tyres. So the Sihouette of 1976 made a virtue of its handicap: tacked-on glassfiber wheelarch extensions.

slant four-cylinder version could be built on the same production line, should the V8 be so successful that sufficient money was generated for Lamborghini to manufacture his own version of the British Mini, which he admired even more than the Fiat 500.

Stanzani designed the new engine for this Urraco, or Little Bull, with ease of servicing in mind, but it still produced 220 bhp in single overhead camshaft form, 30 bhp more than Porsche's rival 911S. Styling was along the lines of the Miura with air conditioning already considered an essential in the American market built into the car from the start, rather than added as an afterthought in the manner of a Porsche. The German manufacturer's synchromesh was adopted in the transmission, however, because it was the best.

The suspension was essentially the same as that used by the British manufacturer Lotus, long renowned for producing the best-handling cars, not only on the road but on the track as well. Such a radical departure from Lamborghini's normal theme needed a lot of development. At that time Porsche was spending at least seven years changing models. Lamborghini tried unsuccessfully to do it in two years, launching the Urraco at the Turin Show late in 1970.

Sad to say, the 2.5-liter needed so much development that it took another two years. By then the world had been hit by its first energy crisis and Porsche had produced its greatest 911, the 210 bhp Carrera RS. This extraordinary car not only killed off Ferrari's Dino, but made life almost impossible for the heavier Urraco.

The Bravo tried to put everything right. It was a startling departure by Bertone from the accepted Urraco theme, bearing a close relationship to the styling ideas pioneered by the Countach.

Hard times and the Silhouette

Virtues such as truly wonderful handling stood little chance against the searing acceleration of the Carrera RS. Stanzani fought back, redesigning the V8 engine as a dramatically improved 265 bhp four overhead camshaft 3-liter, with a 182 bhp 2-liter two overhead camshaft economy version for the Italian market. By then it was 1974 and continuing industrial unrest in Italy led Ferruccio Lamborghini to sell out to a Swiss consortium.

Then, just as the 3-liter Urraco seemed about to take off, Porsche launched the tremendous 300 bhp Turbo. this was a far heavier and more luxurious 911 than the Carrera RS, but it could match the Urraco's 257 km/h (160 mph) and leave it standing on acceleration.

Times change, and black leather is rampant. The interior of a Jalpa reflected how far the management of Lamborghini had to bend to what the customer really wanted: hidebound tradition.

When viewed from the back, the Jalpa (left) reflected its Miura heritage.

Lamborghini never gave up fighting, and tried to emulate the runaway success of the Ferrari 308 — backed by untold millions of lire from Fiat — by producing the Jalpa. It sold only in small numbers, however, as investors concentrated on brand names: Ferrari and Porsche for small cars, Lamborghini for big ones like the Countach.

As receivers moved into Lamborghini, Stanzani moved out and Dallara returned in 1976 as a consultant to rework the Urraco as the Silhouette. These cars sold in small numbers, as Lamborghini thought it had found salvation from a contract with BMW to build a new Silhouette racing car called the M1. The Italian government provided backing, but much of the loan was spent on a dramatic off-road vehicle called the Cheetah, aimed at the Middle East. Sadly, this Chrysler-powered machine with its military potential failed to sell to the big arms manufacturers and buyers.

Eventually, stability returned in 1981 as Lamborghini was taken over by the French Mimram family, and the Silhouette was revised in 270 bhp 3.5-liter form as the Jalpa. It soldiered on providing an alternative to Ferrari's 308 and the Porsche 911 until 1990, alongside a Lamborghini V12-engined Cheetah called the LM002. Throughout this period, however, it was a far more dramatic car that kept Lamborghini alive.

Lamborghini craved the simplicity of the Porsche four-bolt system for retaining a power train, and designed its V8 engine around such principles.

Lamborghini tried to make money by building the Jalpa on a modern production line, but failed because the firm could not charge a high enough price for a car smaller than a Countach.

RUDE WONDER

As the Miura SV went into production in 1971 an even more splendid Lamborghini appeared at the Geneva Show. It was a combination of Stanzani's ideas on how the Miura could be improved, and Gandini's elaboration of a theme first seen in Bertone's Carabo show car of 1968 and the wedge-shaped Lancia Stratos of 1970.

Stanzani was never afraid to take dramatic steps to solve a problems. He had already reversed the engine's rotation in the Miura. Now he swung the entire engine and transmission around so that it was aligned fore and aft rather than across the car. Whereas most designers placed the gearbox behind the engine in such installations to make the driveline more logical, Stanzani did it the other way round. He had the gearbox at the front, with a driveshaft to the rear wheels running through the engine!

His reasons were twofold: the Miura had a tendency to try to take off at high speed, and it had an awkward gearchange. Stanzani realized that he could keep the nose down by moving the weight of the transmission forward and, at the same time, improve the gearchange by eliminating long operating rods. Running a propeller shaft clean through the engine was simple for such an engineer.

Gandini's new body was extraordinary, an ultimate expression of the wedge shape that had

When viewed from high up, the Countach (below left) can be seen to follow the lines established by the ultimate Urraco.

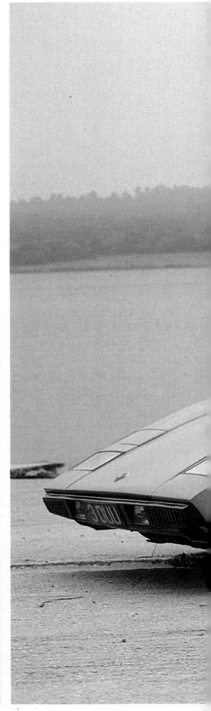

become popular in racing because it made a car more stable. And at last he managed to gain approval for doors that opened upwards like the wings of a beetle (or carabo), by fitting the internal hinges with linchpins so that the occupants could knock them out and extract themselves from the car should they find themselves upside down.

As the car was very much a Bertone project, rather than Lamborghini's, it was the former company that named it: Countach (pronounced Coon-tash'), a Piedmontese expression of rude wonder and amazement.

The doors of a Countach resembled a beetle's wings and gave it the most amazing appearance.

The new Countach S, which presented such a radical departure from accepted practice during the mid-1970s, incorporated glassfiber wheelarch extensions to cover its new, wide tyres.

It certainly set the supercar world alight in 1971 and Bob Wallace was left with the problem of making it work. He was determined that it would be no half-finished masterpiece, so the development took three years. This was not too much of a problems because Lamborghini had plenty of other projects, and the Miura SV was selling well.

Fast and nimble

The prototype Countach LP500 (for Longitudinal Posteriore 5 litri) had a 5-liter version of the existing V12, which had to be reduced to 4 liters for reliability in the LP400 production versions from 1974. Wallace reconstructed the chassis around a spaceframe similar to that used in the Maserati Birdcage racing cars on which he had worked with Alfieri. Weight was kept to a minimum so that the Countach performed well on only 4 liters and proved uncommonly nimble for a car capable of 305 km/h (190 mph). It was to be the old team's last great work before Lamborghini fell upon hard times.

Engine accessability became almost an afterthought on a Lamborghini after the heady days when it was thought that the Urraco could be more practical than a Porsche 911.

The Lamborghini V12 engine was such an advanced concept that 22 years after it was first made, it was found that it could provide competitive power for a Tiga sports racing car, seen here on test at Silverstone.

*Tiff Needell tests the Lamborghini-Tiga.
It became the first of the Spice sports
racers, which went on to win the world
championship.*

When Dallara returned in 1976, he revised it to run on new low-profile tyres in a similar manner to the Silhouette; and he improved the interior and offered optional aerodynamic aids on the Countach S available from 1978. Just as Lamborghini seemed about to collapse, sustained only by the profitable Countach, the Mimrams took over and Alfieri was hired as a consultant to develop a softer and more economical LP500S with a 4.7-liter engine, which was still good for 290 km/h (180 mph).

These cars continued in various forms up to 5 liters as Chrysler took over in 1987 to finance a new supercar that would put Lamborghini back into a class of its own. Gandini was hired to design the Countach replacement with the long-serving Ferrari technical chief Mauro Forgieri, heading an independent company Lamborghini Engineering, based in Modena. He began work on advanced projects for Lamborghini, at the same time designing Grand Prix engines for sale to other manufacturers.

Later the Countach was developed in an LP500 model with a more sophisticated interior (right).

Clean as a clinic: the Lamborghini engine assembly line at Sant'Agata in 1984.

Ultimately the Countach was developed into an anniversary line in 1988 — 25 years after the first Lamborghini was built.

International prospects

Although the resulting Diablo, which replaced the Countach in 1990, was recognized as the work of Gandini, it had been much modified by Chrysler. Gandini then felt free to collaborate in a new car called the Cizeta, produced in California by former Lamborghini engineer Claudio Zampolli with many of the key personnel from the Stanzani—Wallace era. This had a body like the one visualized for the Diablo, with the V16 engine that Ferruccio Lamborghini had always wanted.

Meanwhile the original Lamborghini V12 engine was redesigned for the Diablo with a capacity of 5.7 liters and power output of 485 bhp. The chassis was reworked and plans were made to incorporate a four-wheel-drive system developed by Steyr-Daimler-Puch in Germany, while Chrysler talked to BMW about collaboration along the lines of the M1. From being an Italian wonder, Lamborghinis look like becoming truly international.

The engine bay of the Diablo (left) was basically the same as that of the Countach, although the engine was completely new.

Leather featured strongly in the Diablo interior (left below).

How it all works: an exploded concept drawing of the Diablo, which was to replace the Countach.

Much of the Countach heritage was retained in the Diablo (below).

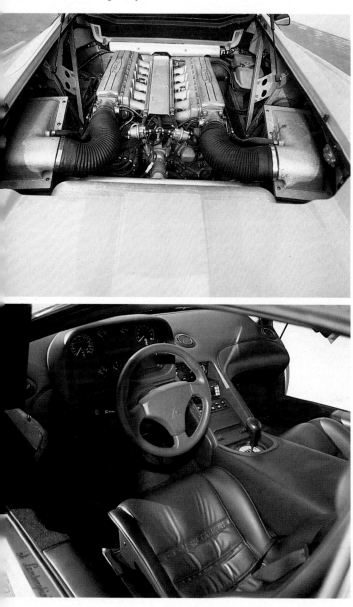

This page: *A 450SLC fixed-head coupé of 1974*

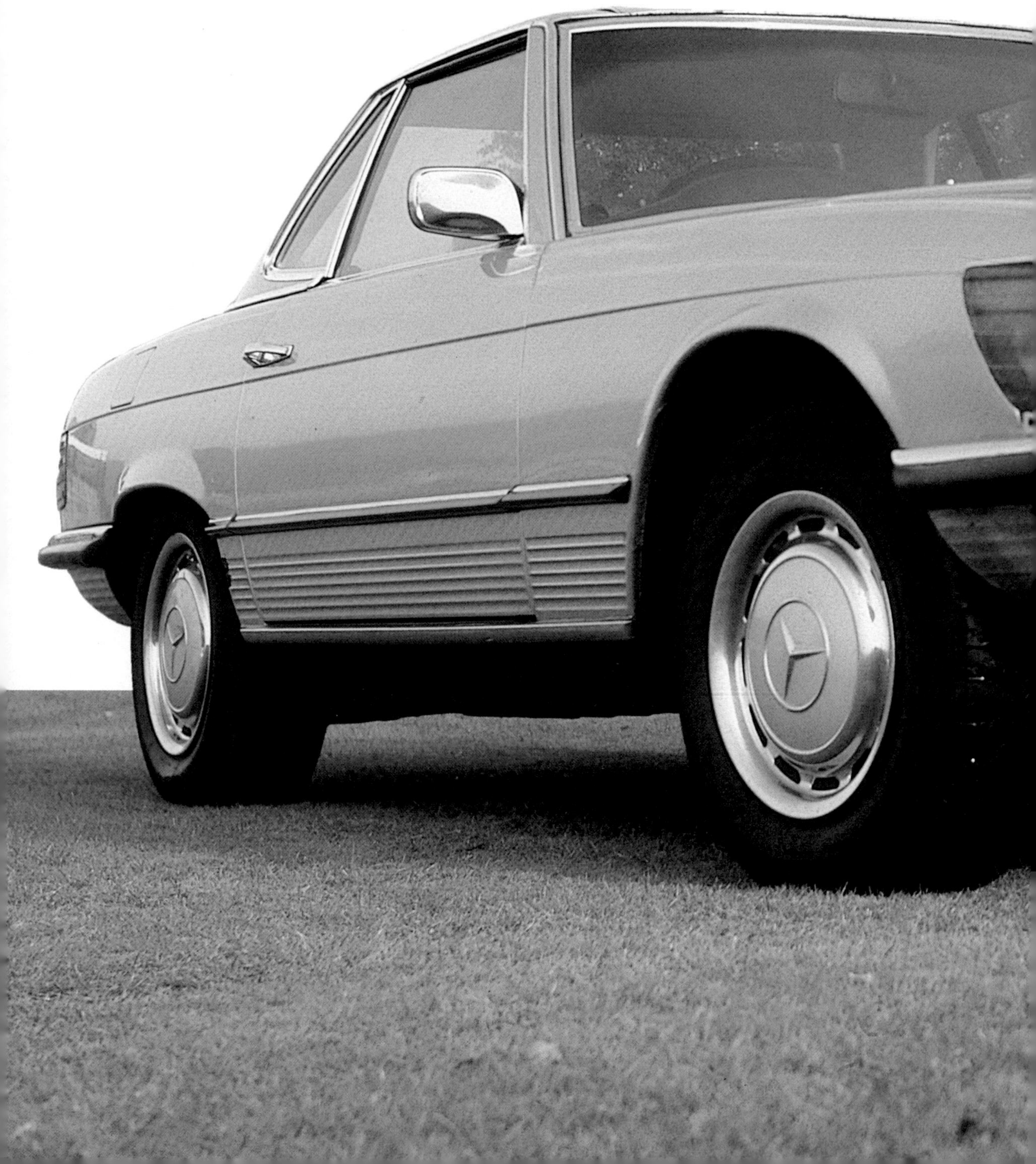

MERCEDES-BENZ

Stuart Bladon

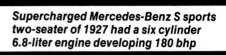
Contents   Page

INTRODUCTION

Daimler and Benz are the names of the great founders of the company which still trades, over a hundred years later, with the same ideals of producing the best cars possible. But where does Mercedes come into it?

It was in 1882 that one of the two founders, Gottlieb Daimler, moved to Bad Canstatt, then a flourishing spa, but now a suburb of Stuttgart, and started to work in a conservatory-workshop in the grounds of his home to improve the four-stroke engine which Nikolaus Otto had invented – hence the Otto cycle. He was helped by Wilhelm Maybach.

Daimler's early achievement (in 1883) was the invention of 'hot tube ignition', a tube protruding through the cylinder wall, and heated by the exhaust gases, to ignite the fuel/air mixture. From this was derived the word *chauffeur*, being the name given (after the French word *chaud*, meaning heat) to the man who warmed up the ignition tubes for his master in the morning when the engine was cold.

Nineteenth-century milestones

In 1885, the first form of car actually ran, when a wooden framed vehicle with this engine chugged through the park

Daimler's villa on 10 November. It was more a form of
motorcycle than a car, since the two main wheels were in
line, with two small ones on outriggers at the side.

The first four-wheelers

A year later came the first true four-wheel car, when
Daimler installed one of his engines in a specially ordered
carriage without horse shafts. In the same year of 1886,
Karl Benz of Mannheim lodged his significant patent for
a vehicle operated by a gas engine . . . whose gas is
generated from vaporizable substances by an apparatus
carried on the vehicle.'

Karl Benz and Gottlieb Daimler worked separately. Each
formed his own business to promote his inventions and the
development of the automobile and, a remarkable fact,
they never met, although they lived only about 60 miles
from each other.

*Daimler-Benz was formed from the merger
of the two separate companies founded by
Gottlieb Daimler and Karl Benz. Water
cooling was used for Benz's first car* (below,
right); *Daimler's first machine* (bottom) *was a
form of motor cycle with outriggers. The
Mercedes name was used by Daimler from
1900;* (below, left), *a splendidly preserved
1904 example*

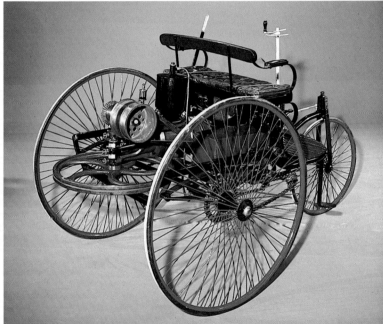

The first Mercedes

An enthusiast for the cars which Daimler produced was the Austrian businessman and consul-general Emil Jellinek, who lived in Nice. He went to Canstatt, saw Daimler, and ordered considerable numbers of his cars, which he sold among wealthy friends and acquaintances on the French Riviera.

In 1899, Jellinek entered a 23 hp Daimler in the touring competition of Nice, and used a pseudonym – Mercedes. It was the name of his pretty ten-year-old daughter. The car won first prize, and when in the following year he ordered 36 of Daimler's latest design, he suggested that the name Mercedes be used for them. It is a Spanish girl's name, and the word means 'mercy'. It was registered as the trade name for the Daimler car in 1902.

Daimler died in 1900, and his two sons carried on the business; it was on their suggestion that both three- and four-pointed stars were adopted as trademarks, but only the three-pointed star was used.

Daimler-Benz is born

In the depression and roaring inflation of 1924 in Germany, automobile manufacturers had difficulty in staying in business. The merger of the then well-established firms of Benz and Daimler was a logical move to ensure survival.

From Benz came the laurel wreath, which had been adopted in 1909 as the company's trademark, replacing the gear wheel which had previously been used. From Daimler came the name Mercedes, which had persisted a the name for all the company cars. Thus came the odd situation in which the company, Daimler-Benz, built cars called Mercedes-Benz, for many years. In 1989, it was rationalized at last and the car division became Mercedes Benz AG.

This Daimler (right) *is generally accepted as the world's first four-wheel car. At Daytona Bay, Florida, the famous Blitzen Benz (below, centre) with Bob Burman covered the flying mile at a record average speed of 141.7 mph. Early beginnings: the 1894 Benz 1½ hp Velo (bottom, right),* and (below) *a Daimler Mercedes of 1913*

Mercedes script on the radiator and the
famous three-pointed star date back to
1909. This six cylinder 7 liter Mercedes of
1924 was known as the Targa Florio

Four-seater Mercedes touring car of 1902-4 (below) is the Mercedes Simplex. (Lower picture): Huge headlamp of a 1904 Mercedes 70 hp. After the 1926 merger of Daimler and Benz, the cars became known as the Mercedes-Benz. 1927 model (right) has twin stars on the radiator shell, as well as the now famous free-standing mascot

Luxury image of the ocean-going liner was appropriately used in Mercedes advertising. An early (1923) six-cylinder supercharged two-seater (top) contrasts with the later (1932) SSK tourer (left)

Introduced in 1927, the supercharged S had a 6.8-liter six-cylinder engine, and led to this 1929 model, the 38/250 TT

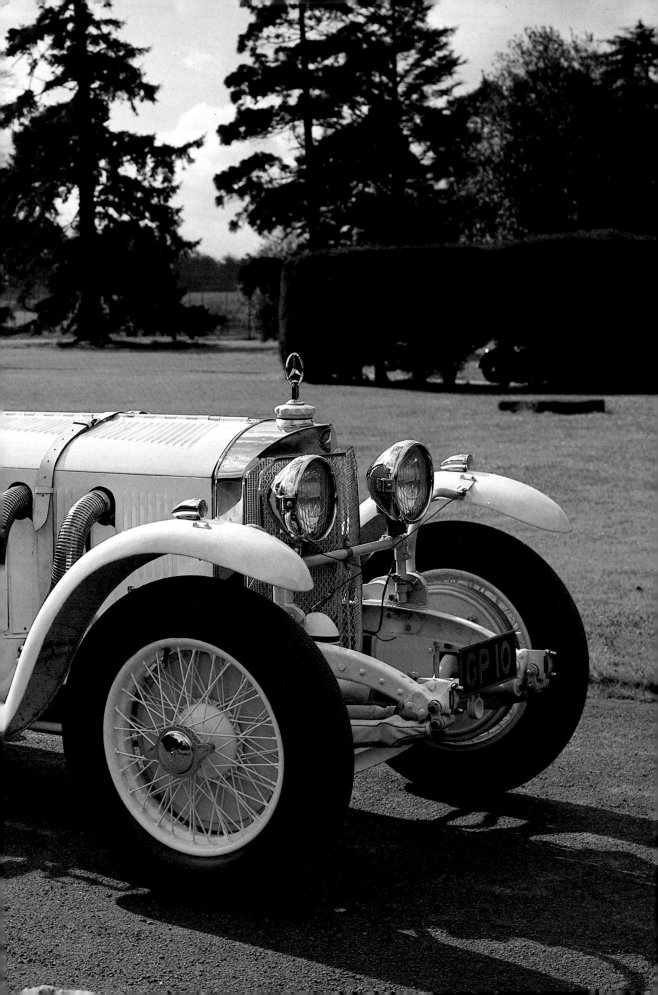

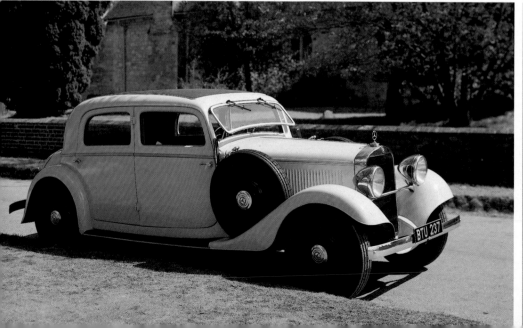

1929 7.2-liter supercharged two-seater (above), and (left) an unusual Mercedes – the mid-engined four-cylinder two-seater sports of 1934. One of the series of "bread and butter" saloons of the 1930s is seen (far left), a 1936 Mercedes-Benz 200

BEHIND THE THREE POINTED STAR

Many people would like to own a Mercedes-Benz, even if they have never driven one and can only imagine what it would be like. Such is the strength of the image the company has developed for itself that perfection is presumed, and taken for granted. Centerpiece of the legend behind the oldest car make in existence is the three-pointed star symbol which graces every model.

On saloons, it stands as a mascot – spring-loaded so that it would not add to the injuries of anyone hit by the car in an accident – and the light glints on its triangular-section arms; on the sports cars it is enlarged, and forms the centerpiece of the grille.

A legend of quality

Strength, reliability, solidity and lasting service, these are the implications of the Mercedes legend; they are the attributes which the Mercedes buyer expects to find, and for which he is prepared to pay generally much higher prices than are asked for rivals of similar size and performance. The buyer is seldom disappointed.

Balance of design, advanced technology and the optimum combination of safety, quality, durability and economy are the basic principles of a successful model policy, say Daimler-Benz. All of these aspects have been, and always will be, the subject of intense research to retain the strengths on which the company has been built up over the years. The quality is evident in the way in which the cars last, and is endorsed by the extensive use of Mercedes saloons for taxi work in so many countries around the world.

Nearly half a billion dollars are spent on research every year. In particular, the Mercedes-Benz car has an unquestioned reputation for safety, won by costly perseverance in crash-testing, accident investigation and research into, for example, seat belts which self-tension in event of an accident, and into development of the chassis for the safest possible handling behavior in an emergency on slippery roads.

Six-cylinder Type 28/95 of 1926, with four-door tourer bodywork. Engine capacity was 7,273 c.c.

Manufacture and export

More than 12 per cent of all cars built in Germany are Mercedes products. Yet the company's strength is partly owed to its long policy of developing overseas markets. Almost half of the cars built, and well over half of the trucks, are exported, and they go to 170 different countries. West Europe, North America and the Middle East are the company's chief markets. The company has its own marketing operation in important export countries.

In an inter-linked production system, Mercedes products are built at 11 factories in Germany. Main assembly is carried out at the two big plants at Stuttgart. One is at the traditional headquarters of the company, called Stuttgart-Unterturkheim, the other at nearby Sindelfingen. Increasing numbers of Mercedes cars are also now being built at the very modern plant at Bremen in the north of Germany, former home of the once-renowned Borgward make. Other plants produce components, such as the one at Düsseldorf which makes steering assemblies.

Outside Germany there are a number of other Mercedes production works and assembly plants, and important

subsidiaries in the United States, Brazil, Argentina and Spain. Around the world, Daimler-Benz employs some 85,000 people.

A very special sort of car

Take a typical day at the Sindelfingen plant, and you find upwards of 1500 people at a reception center at the factory. There's a holiday atmosphere, and wives and children are milling about. What is going on? you may ask. As happens almost every working day, almost 600 brand new Mercedes are being taken away by their new owners.

Not for them the usual routine of train shipment and onward travel by delivery driver. If your new car is going to be a Merc, you go over to Stuttgart to take delivery in person, if you can possibly spare the time. It's that sort of car.

Post-war elegance of style in the 300 Automatic with fuel injection for its 180 bhp engine, new at the London Show in 1957

Famous star, and the laurel wreath emblem inherited from Benz & Cie (far left); 300S four-door convertible (left). Diesels have long been an important part of Mercedes production, and the picture (left corner) shows three generations of diesels: from left of picture, 260D of 1936, 170D of 1949-53, and 200D. (Below): The exciting 300SL of 1956 (see next chapter)

Overleaf: car of the legend: the 300SL "gull wing"

*A particular favorite: the 230SL launched in
1963 (top); its successor was the broader
V8-powered 350SL (above). A V8 engine of
4,520 c.c. capacity powered the 450SE (left)*

The functional yet stylish TE estate (right), available with six-cylinder 3-liter 24-valve engine, shown at Frankfurt 1989. Far right is the 5.6-liter version (560SEC) of the 1984 S-Class coupé (the two-door SEC) shown below

Shown at the top of this page is the Type W123, with engines from 2-liter to 2.8-liter. Rough terrain is not the usual habitat for Mercedes, but the exception to prove the rule was the 280GE Geländewagen (cross-country car) shown below. For the two-door coupé shown (above and right), the choice of engines was 2.3-liter four-cylinder (230CE), 3-liter six-cylinder (300CE) and a 3-liter 24-valve (300CE–24) with a top speed of 147 mph

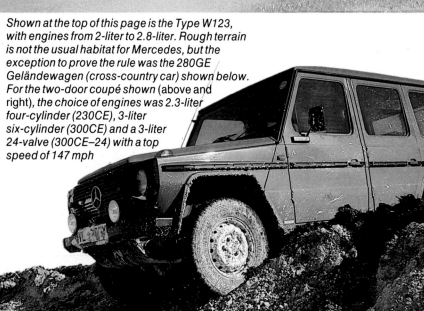

THE LIGHTWEIGHT SPORTS CAR

Although the Mercedes-Benz empire has been built on a marvelous reputation for worth, solidity and longevity, the marque has also consistently been a driver's car. Driver appeal has been exemplified in the sports cars that have backed up the ordinary models of the range. For the past 30 years, they have been given the identity letters 'SL'.

In German the words *Sport Leicht* were used to identify the first of the series – a full translation might be 'the lightweight sports car'. The figures 300 indicated the approximate engine size, as the 300SL which appeared in original racing form in 1952 had a 3-liter six-cylinder engine.

The first SL

On the market early in 1954, the first SL was derived from the car produced to take Daimler-Benz back into motor racing in 1952. The road-going version was again impressively fast, with a top speed of 129 mph, and it would accelerate through the gears to 100 mph in what was then the very quick time of 21.0 seconds.

The six-cylinder engine was unusual in being inclined over to its left side – a layout used by many manufacturers now but rare in the 1950s. Such a layout was made easier by the use of fuel injection instead of carburettors; and that, too, was unusual then among lesser makes, but almost a hallmark of the Mercedes engine.

The most remarkable feature of this first SL was the use of top-hinged doors for its coupé body. Seen from the rear, 300SL with both doors open looked reminiscent of a seagull in flight, and this earned for the SL the nickname Gull Wing. When you opened its heavily curved door upwards, you were confronted with a huge width of sill, and quite an athletic movement was necessary to clamber inside. But things were made easier for the driver by a clever arrangement for the steering wheel to pivot almost to the horizontal, making it easier to get the legs in underneath it.

Much the same body but with much less power was introduced later, having a four-cylinder engine instead of the 3 liter six. Capacity was 1897 cc, and like the 300SL it

Racing version of the SL, the 300SLR won the 1955 Mille Miglia (left). Reason for the "gull wing" name revealed in views of the 300SL (below)

had single overhead camshaft valve gear. Some people decried this model, called the 190SL, and said it was too under-powered; but that disappointment was probably in contrast to the enormous performance of the 300SL.

A bad feature of these and other contemporary Mercedes cars was the rear suspension design. It used an arrangement known as the 'swinging axle', which caused the rear wheels to change their camber angle on bumps and in hard cornering, which upset the handling. In the right hands they could be controlled, as many racing drivers demonstrated, but the inexperienced driver could be caught out by the resultant oversteer on corners.

The refined sports car

'If it's acceptable for the sports saloon, then why not for the sports car as well?' people asked when they noted with surprise the decision of Daimler-Benz to offer power-assisted steering for the new 230SL that was launched in 1963. This new model marked a tremendous advance over the former 190 and 300SLs, although there was no attempt at first to match the 300SL's performance. The 230SL – so named because of its 2.3 liter engine (an overhead camshaft six again) – brought refinement and comfort to the open sports car.

Its hood fitted neatly, and there were frameless glass

e windows. When folded back, the hood disappeared
o a well covered by a hinged panel. The car was a delight
drive, especially when good weather made it possible to
ve the hood down. Especially in automatic transmission
m, the 280SL tended to be under-geared and fussy at
eed, but there were few other faults. Owners could fit a
atly tailored hard-top for the winter. Further refinements
d more power followed, with the introduction of the
der, roomier and still more comfortable 350SL in 1971.
st as the 230SL range had been extended by a choice of
or 2.8 liter engines, so the 350SL became available
er with a six-cylinder 2.8 liter engine, again called the
0SL in spite of the body change. The choice widened,

with arrival of the 4½ liter V8 engine (450SL), and the 350
became the 380SL.

In 1986, this version of the SL went through its final
transition, with the introduction of 5.0- and 5.6-liter V8
engines, plus a 3-liter six-cylinder, bringing back the
famous title '300SL'. Production ended in mid-1989, to
give way to the exciting new SL launched at the 1989
Geneva Show.

300SL Roadster of 1957 (left). *A 300SL
coupé* (below), *and* (lower) *the racing
version, 300SLR*

Rare collection of three 300SLs (above). (Far left and below): Two more well-preserved examples of the coveted 300SL. Power unit was a 3-liter ohc six-cylinder engine with Bosch fuel injection, and the engine was inclined to the left of the car to keep the bonnet height down

Next page: A 1981 coupé version of the SL, a 380SLC

The inviting interior of the 300SL (top left); the steering wheel could be tilted for easier access. As well as the gull wing door model, there was a convertible 300SL (far left). The two-seater convertible of 1982 (left) came with a wide choice of six-cylinder and V8 engines. (Above): A 300SL of 1957 with the 'third generation' SL – the 450SL launched at Geneva in 1973

SL takes on a new meaning: Safety

Advanced technology, safety and style were paramount features of the new generation Mercedes-Benz SL which appeared at the Geneva Show in 1989. Its most advanced safety device is that the onboard computer receives inputs from sensors which detect when 'g' forces become dangerously high and threaten to roll the car over. In this event, the system automatically releases a roll-over safety bar which springs up and gives protection to the occupants.

Soft-top folding is entirely automatic, so that the driver has only to press a button and a sequence of operations is set in train: the header rail catches release; the rear end of the soft-top tips forward to the vertical; the lid of the stowage well opens; the side windows are lowered; the fabric folds down into the well; the well lid closes. The whole sequence takes about 20 seconds, and hey presto! a fully closed car becomes a fully open one. To put the top up, the sequence is reversed. The driver never need leave his seat. A safety device prevents erection or folding of the top unless the speedometer input indicates that the car is stationary.

Engines for the new SL at launch were the six-cylinder 3-liter with 12 valves in one version, another with 24 valves, giving 230 PS, and a 5-liter V8 with 32 valves, giving 326 PS and staggering performance. Many other safety features are standard, including anti-lock brakes. Top speed is governed to 155 mph.

Pictures on this spread show the 500SL in its three forms: fully open, with hood fitted, and with the standard equipment hardtop in position

THE STAR OF LUXURY

Over the years, the Mercedes has always been a relatively expensive car – something to buy as an investment in quality and durability rather than for sheer good value. At the luxury end of the range, there have always been models in the Mercedes line-up to satisfy the most discerning tastes, and to sell to people of great personal wealth or to those with company backing to meet the high investment cost. The Mercedes vies with Rolls-Royce as the natural choice for company chairmen, heads of state and the very rich.

In addition, many Mercedes models have been converted to meet special luxury needs or to be distinctiv

often most extravagant ways. The demand for special Mercedes-Benz bodywork and interior embellishments developed to such extent in the late 1970s and '80s that it as been sufficient to be the main source of livelihood for number of British bodywork specialists.

Custom conversions

Daimler-Benz have always been very reserved about work f this kind. They know it is too important a market for it to e ignored, yet they are wary of suffering claims of dubious eliability as a result of improperly researched modification f their products. When they are asked to approve a onversion, the usual policy is to test and examine and hen, when really satisfied that the work done matches heir own standards, they declare that they 'will not forbid heir dealers to handle it'. This is about as near as they

would ever get to giving official factory approval for major conversion work.

British companies have established a flourishing business with the Middle East, where there is great enthusiasm for luxury cars, a desire to have something distinctive and better than any other; sometimes the most fabulously expensive adaptations have been commissioned.

One of the successful conversions was the ingenious extension of the body of the Mercedes 500SEL to turn it into a limousine. Design was by Le Marquis in the U.K.

Known as the Grosser, the huge 600 was powered by a 6.3-liter V8 engine. The Mercedes star has always been a symbol of quality and luxury

and conversion was undertaken by Tickford of Milton Keynes, a division of Aston Martin.

This conversion is particularly clever for the way in which standard parts are used. A new center pillar is welded in position to the rear of the original one, and a new door is made up each side, using the front part of a rear door and the back part of a front door. This means using the framework of two doors just to make one central door each side, but if you sketch it out on a piece of paper you soon see why this is necessary: the new central door has to mate with the differently shaped fore and aft pillars.

The limousine is offered as a six-door, or the more popular arrangement is that the center door has no exterior handle, and is intended to remain closed for all time. It would not provide very good access to the rear compartment because of the intrusion of the center bulkhead and division, which usually houses television and video.

A word of comfort

Other luxury fittings include a refrigerated drinks cabinet, the most extravagant hi-fi radio and cassette units with multiple speakers and graphic equalizers, radio telephone, and intercom to communicate with the driver. One special Mercedes conversion even had a multiple drinks dispenser allowing rear compartment occupants to dial whatever instant drink they required.

Of special note is the work done by Duchatalet, which has featured at a number of the international motor shows. This consists of magnificent embellishment of Mercedes 500s with the most lavish interior materials, special external decor including gold plating, and the incorporation of every conceivable extra.

The variety of orders is so complex that it needs many individual firms to tackle them. It is small wonder that Daimler-Benz are happy to leave this side of the business to the specialists, including another branch of conversion work in strong demand for some countries – bulletproofing.

Although Daimler-Benz now finish the range with the long-wheelbase 560SEL, with 5.6-liter engine, at one time they produced a huge limousine of their own, the 600. It came in two sizes and was called the Grosse (large). It had only four doors, with central separation and division. Under the bonnet was a huge V8 engine of 6.5-liter capacity.

In place of the enormous 600, a less spectacular but still very impressive limousine continues in production at the time of writing, the long-wheelbase version of the 200 series. With its diesel engine, it is a respected and comfortable 'executive limousine', the sort of car used by many firms for such jobs as taking senior management to the airport.

The 600 limousine was a prestige eight-seater (above left and right). Launched 1980, the Excalibur (left) was designed by Brooks Stevens after the Mercedes 500/540K of 1937-38, and has longer wheelbase. A Chevrolet V8 5-liter hides in the enormous engine compartment

Interior of the 600 Limousine featuring optional television (above, top). In spite of the size of their cars, Daimler-Benz take energy conservation seriously, and evolved an aerodynamic shape for the second generation S-Class (above), launched September 1979. (Right): Special conversion of a 500SE by Panther Cars of Great Britain

Examples of the fascinating conversion work done by Panther Cars of Weybridge, Surrey, England, are seen on these pages. A 500SE gets a very traditional (and highly un-aerodynamic!) radiator grille (right, and below); and (facing page) an extravagant adaptation of 500SLC produces interior in white and red, and gull wing doors. (Lower right): Another luxury interior for a 500SE by Panther.

THE MARQUE OF ACHIEVEMENT

First you could hear the distant roar of the high performance 16 valve engine running at full bore; the noise increased rapidly as it approached. Then came the steadily rising scream of the tires. Finally the car itself was in view for a few seconds – long enough to note the completely different color of the front, black and red with the stains of millions of smashed insects. A sudden crescendo of noise as this ordinary Mercedes-Benz 19 saloon flashed by at over 150 mph. Then, almost as an anticlimax, it was gone, and another circuit of the high-speed bowl of the Nardo proving-ground in southe Italy was completed.

ested to the limit

went on like this for hour after hour, day and night, for
ore than a week. At the end of it, the three Mercedes
0E 16 valve saloons had broken three world speed and
stance records. This was a remarkable achievement of
gh-speed endurance in conditions of extreme
mperature, reaching 104°F (40°C) and rising to 120°F
0°C) inside the car.

For Daimler-Benz this adventure in the summer of 1983
as nothing new. The company has a long history of
cord-breaking and pioneering work setting the pace for
e world's cars. One of the earliest of such enterprises
ok place in America in 1895, when the *Times Herald*
fered $5000 cash prize for a race of 'horseless vehicles'
om Milwaukee to Chicago.

Oscar Mueller driving a Benz and Frank Duryea driving
ar of his own make were the chief contenders. Other

competitors complained that they were not ready by race
day. Duryea crashed, leaving Mueller to win, covering the
92 mile course in just under 9½ hours. The main event had
been postponed to give competitors longer for preparation,
and this time Mueller was second, winning $1500. In the
same year six Daimler-powered cars were among the first
eight in the famous Paris-Bordeaux-Paris race, two of
them being Benz cars.

*Record-breaking 190E 16V at the Nardo
proving ground in southern Italy* (left). *The
last year up to start of World War I in 1914
produced this 117 racer* (below, upper) *and
saw Daimler win the GP of France and the
Vanderbilt race in America.* (Lower): *Another
Grand Prix car (1914) which has been
preserved and restored*

Postwar victories

A sizable book could be filled with the endless saga of
Daimler-Benz racing victories through the years, including
a series of triumphs when the company resumed racing in
1952. Less well remembered, perhaps, but still significant,
was the catalog of international rally successes which
Mercedes cars won in the late 1950s and early '60s.

During the notoriously testing Liège-Sofia-Liège rally of
1963, at a rally control in Yugoslavia, the marshal took a
ruler and drew a line across his chart with the passing of
every minute without arrival of any competitors. Suddenly
the squat, purposeful shape of the Mercedes 230SL came
roaring into view and skidded to a halt in a cloud of dust. It
was some minutes before anyone else came in, and the
230SL driven by Bohringer and Kaiser arrived back at
Liège looking travel-stained but unmarked – a clear winner

When the promising new Wankel rotary engine burst
upon the motoring scene in the early 1960s, Daimler-Benz
devoted immense effort to development of the new engine
They never put it into production, but its potential as a
compact but powerful engine was illustrated by a special
two-seater sports car, the C111. It appeared first with a
three-rotor Wankel engine in 1969, and was then shown at
Geneva in 1970 with a four-rotor Wankel, equivalent to a
4.8 liter conventional piston engine. The same special

ports car was later used to demonstrate speed and endurance for existing piston engines. A supercharged ve-cylinder 3 liter diesel engine was fitted, which set new world records for diesel cars at the amazingly high speed of 157.4 mph for 10,000 miles.

Later, a Mark IV version of the legendary C111 was fitted vith a V8 petrol engine with twin turbochargers, and chieved the fantastic speed of 403.9 km/h (251 mph).

The most extraordinary record of all was set by an erodynamic Daimler-Benz economy special. This car nanaged 2875 miles per gallon of diesel fuel on the lockenheimring motor-racing circuit.

The 1937 Type W125 Grand Prix car had eight cylinders in line in two batches of four, with four valves per cylinder. It was supercharged, and developed nearly 650 bhp from capacity of 5,660 c.c. (left and below). Caracciola won the European drivers' championship for the third year running in the W154 (bottom), which had a V12 3-liter engine with twin overhead camshafts for each bank of six cylinders, working four valves per cylinder – a total of 48 valves! It had twin superchargers and developed 450 bhp

Mercedes embarked on a return to Grand Prix racing in 1952, and won six major races in 1954. Here is Hermann Lang in the Type W196

In 1988, Mercedes-Benz took the daring decision to go back
into motor sport, and the first really big test came in the Le
Mans 24-hour race in June 1989 (below). The aerodynamic
Sauber-Mercedes attained 250 mph on the Mulsanne
straight, and won the race at an average speed of 137.49
mph, driven by Jochen Mass/Manuel Reuter/Stanley
Dickens. In September 1989, the Sauber-Mercedes team
took the first two places at Donington, and clinched the world
sport-prototype championship with two races still to go. Inset
is a1955 300SL in the 1984 Mille Miglia commemoration run

Below: *During the final year of 911 production, Porsche reverted to the time-honored, Beetle-browed Speedster for one of its optional body styles on a Carrera base*

Next page: *Porsche took the Turbo further upmarket with a special slant-nosed version using similar styling to that of the 935 racing cars*

PORSCHE

Chris Harvey

Contents	Page

INTRODUCTION

Generations come and generations go, but Porsche sporting cars seem to go on forever. Their timeless appeal can only be seen as a tribute to the genius who inspired them, Professor Ferdinand Porsche.

Early days

Previously, Professor Porsche had designed all manner of machines, culminating in the first Volkswagen people's car in 1936. By the 1930s, Professor Porsche was running his own design studio, producing blueprints for everything from racing cars to tanks.

Germany was his adopted home, and there Hitler was persuaded to let his studio produce a glamorous competition version of the austere Volkswagen for the Berlin-to-Rome Axis race in 1939. The race never happened, but two of the team cars survived as an inspiration for the Porsche family to set up a new manufacturing company a Gmund, in their native Austria, after the war. Times were hard and they made their first cars from spare parts, mos from old Volkswagens.

The first car to bear the name Porsche was designed b the professor's son, Dr Ferdinand Porsche, along lines la out by his father, who was by then more than 70. Its Volkswagen engine was reversed to lie ahead of the rear

wheels and carried in a tubular frame, a layout that can still be seen today in racing Porsches. Their second car, with a similar Volkswagen Beetle-like body, had the engine in the familiar place behind the rear wheels to make more room for touring – a configuration that survives today in the classic Porsche 911 series.

The Spyders are coming

From these first cars in 1947, hundreds of combinations have been tried on similar themes.

The old Professor lived long enough to see high-performance versions of the touring cars win their class in the Le Mans 24-hour race in 1951 as they established themselves in rallying at the same time. The publicity helped sell the production cars, and never since then have Porsche been out of competition. Ultra-light versions of the mid-engined design had skimpy open bodies and adopted the Italian name Spyder, which had originated on horse-drawn racing carriages that darted along like insects. Competition coupés with the same high-revving

The earliest 1100cc coupé (far left top), with its rear-mounted engine and Volkswagen-style platform chassis, was easily distinguished by its money-saving split windscreen. The same basic layout was carried through, with four-wheel drive, to the ultimate 959 (below), leaning heavily on technology developed on the 956, seen in the pits in 1984 (far left below). The 956 stuck to the mid-engined format established by the very first Porsche

engines were soon called Carreras after early success in the Carrera Panamericana road race in Mexico. Such victories helped establish an even bigger market for Porsche on the US West Coast than in Europe.

The Spyders were developed to such an extent that they could go grand prix racing in open-wheeled form in the early 1960s. New engines were built as a result with even more power, and open sports cars dominated the last of the great road races, the Targa Florio in Sicily. At the same time, the basic production cars were becoming faster and more luxurious to meet market demand. Work on the 911 series started as early as 1956, with the first version seen in 1963.

The sports racing cars became ever faster, until the awesome 917 hit 240 mph at Le Mans and needed drivers of the highest caliber to control it. Eventually these incredible cars became more manageable even when they were turbocharged to stay ahead of the opposition. Such work soon found its way into the 911 series for today's Porsche Turbo, which won the world's fastest car title in Britain in 1984. Open versions of the 911 took the name Targa, and ultimately Cabriolet and Speedster.

Like dinosaurs, the 917s had to die, but their spirit survived in scaled-down versions that took a string of wins at Le Mans, evolving into today's all-conquering 956 and 962 endurance racers.

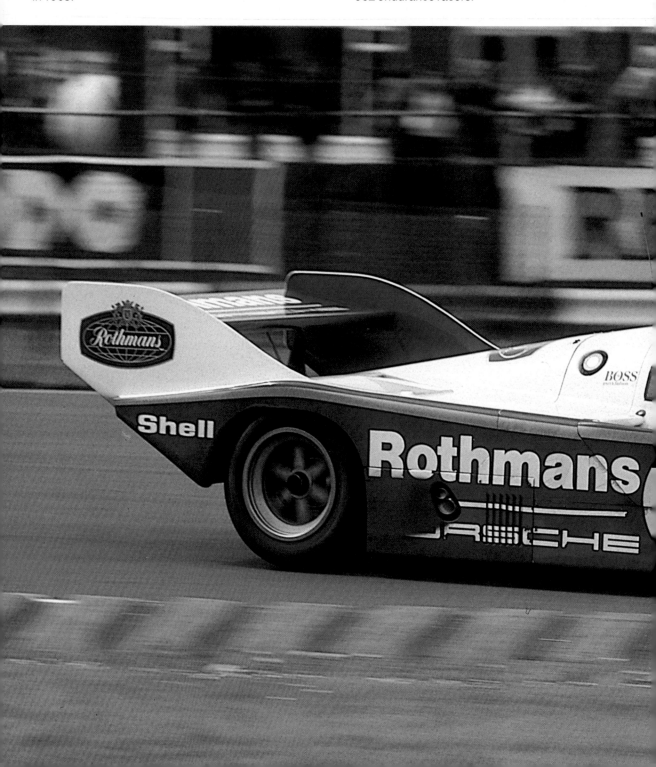

High technology

By the middle of the 1970s Porsche were strong enough to survive the world oil crisis that spelled financial doom to many makers of luxury goods. But not before they had gone back to their roots to produce another Volkswagen-based cheap sports car, the 914. This philosophy was carried over into the base-line 924 series of front-engined Porsches, and into today's complementary 928 and 944 luxury sports coupés.

Porsche have never stopped designing things. Their studio has been responsible for all manner of high-technology products, including a formula one engine that powered the highly successful McLaren grand prix cars. Truly, Porsche have become *the* sporting car maker for all seasons, with the same family still in control, headed by Dr Ferdinand Porsche.

The 956 has been all-conquering in world endurance championship racing, particularly in the hands of Belgian Jacky Ickx, usually partnered by Germany's Jochen Mass, or the Briton Derek Bell. Ickx and Mass's works 956 is pictured here at Silverstone, UK, in 1983.

THE FAMOUS BEETLE MARCHES ON

The first Porsches were kept as simple as possible to make production easier, a fact highlighted by the designation, 356, their original planning code. These models might have had no name at first, but they soon established a character for Porsche that has not deserted the marque: they were of superb quality despite the early piecemeal methods of production. They were also fast because they had highly streamlined bodies and held the road well if the driver was good enough to cope with so much of the weight at the back. If the driver was not so good, the car handled like a pendulum, with the tail swinging from side to side. This strange ability, or lack of it, meant that you either loved the car for the nimble way it could be induced to negotiate tight corners, or hated it because you couldn't control it – factors that have stayed with the rear-engined variants of the marque to this day.

One of the reasons for putting the engine so far back, apart from leaving more space in the passenger compartment, was that it gave the Porsches superb traction on rough roads, of which there were many in Europe just after the war. Porsches still show an amazing ability to climb hills.

The earliest 356s were almost invariably fixed-head coupés because they were meant for quiet, well-insulated touring, although a few more expensive but very civilized convertibles were made along similar lines.

It was natural that Porsche should retain close links with Volkswagen because they still held patents on many of the German car's features. All the early 356s used Volkswagen running gear, modified for better performance. It was partly for this reason that they proved to be very reliable, another factor that has contributed so much to the marque's enviable reputation.

By 1950 demand was high enough for Porsche to start a move back to their old headquarters in Stuttgart. The move was not an easy one; the works were occupied by the US forces' motor pool. However, already the Volkswagen was selling well in America and it was not difficult for an Austrian-born car importer, Max Hoffman, to start selling them as a sporting version of the Beetle. By 1954 he was taking a third of Porsche's production, and later American sales reached 70 per cent.

Throughout these early years, the Porsche engineers behaved like all Porsche engineers have done since – they

The distinctive style of the bubble-topped Volkswagen Berlin-to-Rome racer (below right) formed the basis for the 356 body, which was subsequently marketed as the Speedster with no top at all. These Beetle-like open cars (left and bottom right) have now become a prized item in any US collection.

could not resist making improvements to their cars, no matter how painstaking. In major ways, the engine was enlarged from 1100 cc to 1500 cc in easy steps, and a special version for competition offered as an option. Windscreens became one-piece as soon as the tools to make them could be bought, and even the old throttle-cable was replaced with a more reliable rod.

In 1954 Porsche began making special models for America, with one of the most emotive being the chop-topped Speedster, a lightweight sports car that appealed to fresh-air fanatics.

These cars were also attractive to a vocal minority because they were so light, but there was not much profit margin because they had no luxury fittings. Porsche were quick to identify this problem and saw a better future in more luxurious sports cars. They had no intention of expanding into mass-production where they would have had to compete with established giants. So that was the end of the Speedster.

The new philosophy

The models that followed, the 356A, 356B and the 356C, were the results of constant development on the original theme. But there came a point where no more power could be extracted from a normal engine to give either more performance or the same when the weight of even more luxurious fittings had to be hauled along. It was also apparent that the 356 had to be made bigger to cope with a population of ever-increasing physique.

Work had been going on for years on the car to replace the 356, the 911, which eventually went into production in 1964. The last of the 356s continued to be produced alongside it until orders for the new model built up to such a degree that Porsche could concentrate on the 911. But that last 356, the Carrera 2, was a wonderful car descended straight from the racers that dominate the next chapter.

The light weight of the Speedster (below) *soon made it an attractive proposition for competition along with the Carrera versions of the standard coupé. The fastest of the 356s was the last, the Carrera 2* (right and over page), *with a full two-liter four-cam racing engine. It was gradually modified until it reached C-specification in the 1964 model.*

To the purist's eye, the type 356A, pictured in silver Super 75 1600 cc form (below and left inset), presented one of the cleanest and least-cluttered early Porsche forms . . . with the Carrera 2 (right inset) presenting an emotive ending to the early part of the Porsche story.

THE ORIGINAL RACERS

From the start, all Porsches were designed to be able to acquit themselves well in competition, even if that was not their primary purpose. But some *were* designed purely for racing or rallying, with any form of touring ability as an incidental bonus. These cars had a dual function in that they provided not only publicity for the marque, but a constant feedback of information on how new ideas fared in the most extreme circumstances. The usual progression of development on these mobile test beds was more power, followed by better handling to cope with it.

The Berlin-to-Rome Axis prototype never made a race, but the first open car that bore the name Porsche did. It was sold to a Swiss customer called Kaes, who promptly won his class in a race at Innsbruck in 1948.

After that a succession of customers, often wealthy Austrian or German noblemen, took the early Gmund alloy-bodied coupés to victory in racing and rallying, notably Prince Joachim zu Furstenberg in the Swedish Midnight Sun Rally in 1950 and later Baron Fritz Huschke von Hanstein in all manner of events. But it was not until Le Mans in 1951 that the factory could afford to compete officially and then they immediately won their class with a coupé!

German Volkswagen dealer Walter Glockler had cut the top off one of the Gmund coupés, reducing the weight even further for short-distance events in which aerodynamics

The Spyders (below) featured a tubular chassis called a space frame – because, when viewed as a whole, there is more space between the tubes than area of metal – like that on the first Porsche, with, initially, a skimpy open body and later, by 1964, when Jo Bonnier was pictured (right) competing in the Targa Florio, a much-modified version featuring a rear spoiler.

were of lesser importance, and subsequently sold it to Hoffman, eventually giving rise to the Speedster cult. Glockler was then to enjoy a great deal of support from the works with a series of specials based on frames like that used by the first Porsche. These frames were lighter and stronger than the normal platform chassis, but cost a lot more to make, so they did not find their way into production cars. But just about everything else on these 'spyders' did. The engine capacity was increased to 1500 cc, and these units doubled up for the coupés – which kept the normal chassis.

The Spyders were then developed by the factory into the legendary Type 550, which was capable of 140 mph.

A new engine

Coupés were most frequently used for tiring races like the Carrera Panamericana, but it was to be a 550 that won its class in this event in 1953. By that time the 1500 cc pushrod engine was at the peak of its development, so Porsche produced another power unit, with four overhead cams and far more potential. The Spyder then became known as the 550/1500RS, for *Rennsport,* or circuit racing. Notable victories included class wins in the classic Italian road race, the Mille Miglia, in 1954 and at Le Mans.

Technical development ran riot and Porsche Spyders soon received five-speed gearboxes, which subsequently found their way into road cars, and even four-cam engines for coupés called Carreras. By 1956 the number of modifications to Spyders were reflected in their designation, Type 550A/1500RS, which was frequently cut down to RS. Their name might have been long-winded, but they won races such as the 1956 Targa Florio for Umberto Maglioli.

Continuous development led to a version called the RSK in 1957, the K describing the shape of its new front suspension; the swing-axle rear suspension was also

replaced with a more sophisticated coil spring system, and the works cars became fast enough to challenge for the overall lead in top races like Le Mans.

The grand prix route

When they were stripped down, the sports cars also proved competitive in the new formula two, normally reserved for open-wheeled racing cars. Carreras won the Liege-Rome-Liege rally in 1957 and 1959; more highly developed versions of the RSK, called RS60s, won sports car events in 1960; and open-wheeled variants took first and second place in the German Grand Prix for Jo Bonnier and Wolfgang Count Berghe von Trips.

Porsche were suitably encouraged to build a formula one car, powered at first by the four-cylinder, four-cam engine – with which American hero Dan Gurney took third place in the 1961 world championship – and eventually a new eight-cylinder engine for 1962. This proved too expensive, and Porsche quit formula one, although lightweight Carreras with Italian Zagato bodies raced on with great success until at least 1964.

In sports racing and hill-climbing, the RS60's successor, the RS61, became the W-RS with a blend of Zagato nose and Spyder rear bodywork. These cars were later known as Type 718s after their engine serial and eventually their two-liter four-cammer found its way into the 356 Carrera to produce the formidable Carrera 2.

The Porsche Spyder's timeless shape disguises its age, which is revealed to the keen eye by such period features as steel wheels in place of the alloy ones that have become a standard fitting on modern machinery.

Corrado Cupellini is pictured here racing his Porsche Spyder, the designation RS60 indicating that it was built in 1960.

The first Porsche (top left), with its primitive split windscreen, was a Spyder, the shape changing very little by the time racing machines had reached the 550RS design with their distinctive rear engine ventilation grilles (bottom left). The first major change to the competition Porsche's appearance was when they went open-wheeled for grand prix racing. Jo Bonnier is seen here (right) competing in the British grand prix at Aintree in 1962 with his car featuring the prototype eight-cylinder engine (inset) – surmounted by the typical Porsche cooling fan – that formed the basis of the production 911 power unit.

Porsches became popular in all forms of competition as was demonstrated by this Carrera in the 1964 Monte Carlo Rally (far-left). The formula two car (above), and the RS61 Spyder, pictured racing in 1975 (left), shared the same four-cam engine in differing states of tune.

THE CAR FOR ALL SEASONS

The 911 has to be seen as the car that even Porsche could not kill. It was a long time, seven years, in the making, and since then has given every indication of being immortal. In 1972 it seemed to have reached a peak that could not be surpassed with the fabulous Carrera RS, introduced nine years after the first model was shown. There were factions at Porsche who were convinced that it would have to be replaced by a newer car, one of their projected front-engined series. But such was the continuing demand for 911s that the later cars have never been able to oust it in the sales race. In the 1980s the 911, in turbocharged, normally aspirated and four-wheel drive forms, has found a new lease of life. It is being produced in fully-open form, with the most advanced technology, to keep it at the front as an all-time classic.

Like the 356, the 911 was effectively designed by Dr Ferdinand Porsche. When pressed by advisers to make it a much bigger car than the 356, one that might compete with the likes of Mercedes in the saloon car field, he produced a

saying straight out of Austrian folklore: 'Shoemaker, stick to your last.' He meant that Porsche had been successful by confining their manufacturing efforts to sports cars that were like no others.

The greatest Porsche?

In the established family tradition Dr Ferdinand's son, also called Ferdinand, designed a timeless body only slightly larger than that of the 356 outwardly, but a lot roomier inside. It had a front luggage compartment that was big enough to take a set of golf clubs, and very wide doors, which pleased the Americans. But like the 356, it was built on a platform chassis with an air-cooled engine mounted at the rear. Dr Porsche did not want to change his basic product that much.

It was introduced as the 901, although that designation was soon changed to 911 to avoid conflict with Peugeot, whose models had long had a zero in the middle of their names. And it continued with every conceivable variation on its new flat six-cylinder engine, based on that used in the earlier grand prix cars. At first, a capacity of two liters was

enough, with a high-performance version, the 911S, as an option. Soon after, production cars were built with Targa tops, which had a distinctive built-in polished alloy roll cage aimed at meeting anticipated American legislation against the completely open car. These 911s, in fixed-head and Targa forms, had ever-increasing engine capacities, through 2.2 liters to 2.4 and ultimately 2.7 for lightweight versions called the Carrera RS. They were built to qualify Porsches for production car racing and became wildly popular as road cars, much to Porsche's surprise.

To many enthusiasts, the 2.7 Carrera RS is still the ultimate Porsche, with its combination of superb performance – up to 150 mph – and lithe handling as a result of its low weight. After that, the 911s became heavier, partly because American safety laws meant that

The early 911s – below is a 1967 S model with its special 'five-star' alloy wheels – were light and lithe machines running on relatively narrow tires.

American safety regulations meant that it was not viable for Porsche to market a fully-open version of the 911 (above) until 1982, when it was decided that compulsory roll cages like those featured on the Targa were an infringement of civil liberties. Safety campaigners won one notable victory, however: from 1974, much larger bumpers had to be fitted, as on the red coupé left. This inevitably meant that all subsequent 911s were heavier

they had to have substantial bumpers. But it was partly because there was still more money to be made from very luxurious cars, and by 1975 the fastest 911 was a turbocharged version called the 930, which looked quite different from a normal 911. The wheels were wide and the bodywork arches were taken from a road-racing 911 called the Carrera RSR. Everybody knew the 930 was a 911 at heart, so the conflict was resolved by calling it the Porsche Turbo. It was such a fast and exotic car, however, that most people thought it was the 911's swansong. Surely not even Porsche could develop it further?

But develop it they did, and in 1982 the first fully-open 911, the Cabriolet, was introduced alongside the Targa and fixed-head coupé, which – with uprated 3.2 liter engine – took the name Carrera. When the coupé was fitted with a 962 racing-style engine, four-wheel drive, and even more aerodynamic bodywork, it became the fabulous limited-edition 959. Much of the same technology was then used in a new four-wheel drive Carrera 4 for the 1990s, and in the 911's official replacement, a two-wheel drive version called the Carrera 2.

The close affinity between competition Porsches and their road-going relatives was never better demonstrated than when the bodyshell of the 1974 Carrera RSR and much of its running gear was used as the basis of the Turbo road car in 1975. Subsequently this classic wide-wheeled shape has remained substantially unaltered in the latest Turbos.

One of the delightful aspects of the Porsche 911 and all its variants is the functional nature of every fitting. The bumpers of the blue 1978 911SC (left) retract on hydraulic rams under minor impact, while the driver's mirror of the 1980 SC in white 'Martini' livery (top) is electrically adjustable from the cockpit; and all current Porsche 911s have the very effective headlamp washers pictured on the 1975 Turbo (above).

The Turbo was built initially to qualify a derivant of the 911, the 934, in grand touring races. This form of competition was governed by rules which stipulated a minimum weight – with the result that the 934 competed virtually unaltered from road form, making it one of the most luxurious racing cars ever built.

The definitive shape of the 911 has remained unchanged since 1963 with only minor modifications, such as the optional 'picnic table' rear spoiler to improve stability at high speeds (left inset) and the Targa top as fitted to the example from Germany (right inset), which also featured 935-style front wings.

Aerodynamics play a vital part in the
performance of a car like the Turbo, capable
of more than 160 mph. Despite the confusing
mass of regulations imposed by countries
throughout the world, Porsche have
managed to keep the frontal aspect of the
car (left) as clean as possible, although they
have had to fit the large spoiler at the back
(above) as standard on the Turbo because of
its high performance.

The Turbo-style front air dam with its brake cooling ducts can be seen clearly on the red 911 competing in a classic hill climb (left), while the yellow 2.4-liter Targa (top) has been fitted with a later type Turbo rear spoiler. The graphics of the rear logo are typical of the early 1970s and had given way to a far less pronounced script on the red Turbo (above) by the time it took the World's Fastest Car title in Britain in 1984.

THE FABULOUS RACING PORSCHES

Before 1964, Porsche were very much the underdogs in international sports car racing. They fielded relatively small cars that, although they almost invariably won their classes, were rarely in contention for outright victory. The Targa Florio was a notable exception, being run on such a tortuous course that the larger, heavier, sports racing cars were left behind by the smaller, nimbler Porsches. The long mountain climbs that were popular in Europe also developed into a battleground between Porsche and Ferrari (with their Dinos) because this form of competition was limited to a two-liter capacity. In addition, Porsche did well in races for grand touring cars because their standard product was highly competitive when it did not have to face purpose-built racers.

It was in this area that Porsche started to reach for the top with the 904 in 1964. It was an exceptionally pretty mid-engined machine styled by the third Ferdinand Porsche that astounded everybody by taking second place in the Monte Carlo Rally in 1965 – on snow-covered roads that were a complete contrast to the normal sun-kissed tarmac found in the GT events. The 904's technology was carried over into the 906 in 1966 with the engine capacity also starting to rise, from 2 liters to 2.2; a lighter Type 910 was built along the same lines to win the European Mountain Championship. As a further development of the 910, the Type 907 – Porsche designations can be very confusing – was able to run as high as fifth overall at Le Mans, alongside ultra-lightweight 911s called the 911R.

After that, variants of the 911S had three golden years in international rallying as the 907 turned into the 908 with a three-liter, eight-cylinder engine. These early 908s came within an ace of winning the world sports car champion-ship, with an even lighter Type 909 Bergspyder (mountain spyder) supreme in the hills.

Taming the monster

From the 908 and 909 sprang the 908/2, followed by the 908/3, one of the most successful Porsche sports racing cars ever built. These three-liter prototypes were so successful that international racing regulations were rewritten to allow series production cars to compete on equal terms with engines up to five liters. Porsche replied in 1969 by building enough of their fabulous 917 models to qualify for the larger category. These exotic cars were based on the 908/3, with a twelve-cylinder version of the eight-cylinder engine. It was of 4.5 liters capacity at first

Below: a classic shot of the American specification 962 endurance racer

although it eventually went up to 5.4 liters. With so much power and highly streamlined bodies, they could be lethal at speeds of up to 240 mph before they were tamed by an English engineer called John Horsman. He capitalized on the 908/3's aerodynamics where computers had failed.

By 1973 turbocharged variants of the 917, producing up to 1100 bhp, were dominating American car racing as the fleet 908/3s continued to win races.

The world oil crisis and soaring development costs outlawed the 917. Porsche then concentrated on GT racing with the new 2.7 Carrera RS. This was enlarged to 3. liters before being turbocharged, like the 917, to make the 934 production racer and 935 prototypes. At the same time, the 908 was developed with 917 technology to make the open 936 prototypes that won Le Mans with the 935s into the 1980s.

Once again world endurance racing regulations had to be rewritten as every event was in danger of becoming a Porsche walk-over – at speeds approaching 200 mph! But even in the last year of the old-style racing, 1981, a replica 917, introduced 12 years earlier, was still competitive.

Titles galore

Fuel economy was the watchword of the Group C racing that replaced these events in 1962, and Porsche promptly produced their first full monocoque car, the 956. This was just as successful as its predecessors, winning world titles before being updated as the 962, which continues to be a mainstay of endurance racing.

Meanwhile Porsche developed four-wheel drive versions of the 911 to win the Paris–Dakar desert rallies, culminating in the 959 production version. They also designed world championship grand prix engines for the British McLaren team and ultimately produced a successful Indianapolis-style racing car for America with another British team, March.

Porsche were prone to prepare special Spyders with truncated bodywork for the tortuous roads of the Targa Florio road race in Italy (left). As Porsche were developing their racing cars, they did not neglect prototype work on the road-going models. The red coupé (inset) may look like a 911, but it is one of the rarer-than-rare 901s produced only in September 1964 before the designation was changed. Racing cars continued to have their own numbering system – with the type 907 as one of the most successful (below).

The 917 was only made really manageable when the British engineer, John Horsman, was helping run the blue-and-white Gulf-liveried cars (inset). He cut off the tail to improve high-speed handling, with the Porsche factory adopting the same style – sometimes with fins (left) – as the Gulf cars' lap times tumbled.

The early lightweight 911 R racing Porsche (below) *was built with right-hand drive for more accurate placing on circuits which are predominantly right-handed. By 1978, the Porsche 911 had reached its most extreme shape in the long-nosed and long-tailed 935* (right), *the body panels of which were simply tacked on to a standard shell! Meanwhile Jochen Mass, Australian Vern Schuppan, and American Hurley Haywood, were to race the last of the space-frame spyders, the* 936 (far right), *at Le Mans in 1981.*

By 1984, Porsche were back in formula one racing with Niki Lauda winning the British grand prix at Brands Hatch in his McLaren (below), after Jacky Ickx had taken the marque to a double world title on the same track – but in pouring rain – with the 956 in 1982 (bottom). Later developments of the 956, such as the 962 pictured during a dramatic pit stop at Le Mans in 1984 (right), continued to contest the great sports car races

Some Porsches had a very long life in competition, the 908 pictured in 1983 having been built 12 years earlier! And the glorious old 2.7 Carrera RS from 1972 was still highly competitive in events as rough as the East African Safari rally in 1978 (inset).

PORSCHES FOR THE PEOPLE

No sooner had the Type 356 ended production and the 911 been established than it was apparent that Porsche needed a cheaper sports car to protect their sales from erosion at that end of the market. Initially they hoped that this need would be fulfilled by the Type 912, a 911 with the lower-priced four-cylinder 356 power unit.

It was soon apparent that the 912 could only be a stopgap because it cost almost as much to make as the 911, and Porsche did not have the facilities then to produce enough really cheap cars to show a good return on the money invested. So they did a deal with Volkswagen. The old friends were to produce a sports car that could double up as a Porsche with a high-powered engine, or as a Volkswagen with cheaper running gear. It would be

mid-engined because that seemed to be the way to go at that time; virtually every racing car had this layout by the late 1960s.

A complete change

The 914 that resulted was not a great success, partly because of a changing political situation at Volkswagen which meant that the bodies cost Porsche too much to make their version significantly cheaper than the 911, and partly because of uninspired styling, influenced by American safety dictates. It was also a question of image. Volkswagen, as it turned out, did not have a sporting appeal in Europe, and Porsche, to the Americans, meant pure-bred grand touring car.

Volkswagen saw the 914's boxlike appearance as the chief problem and commissioned Porsche to design a new cheap sports car for them. This would be a far prettier

coupé, using a large number of basic Volkswagen mechanical parts to keep down the price. Volkswagen did not mind Porsche working on a far more luxurious car at the same time; the benefits would be mutual if their appearance was similar. Volkswagen owners would want to gear up to the new expensive Porsche, and Porsche could spread out some of the development costs over both cars.

But once again the political situation changed at

Below: Porsche did not neglect their front-engined range even though the world continued to cry out for the traditional rear-engined 911. They continually updated the 944 until a fully-open cabriolet version became available in 1989

Volkswagen, and the design for the new cheap sports car was dropped, only for Porsche to decide to produce it themselves. They had opted for water-cooled engines because their existing air-cooled units were noisy with no coolant to absorb the sound, and this was expected to become a problem with German legislation in particular. It was also felt necessary to concentrate a large mass of metal at the front of the car to meet ever more stringent American crash laws. So the new machines were front-engined as well as water-cooled, quite unlike the traditional Porsches. But they retained rear-wheel drive in the interests of the best handling and steering.

The most pressing need was for the cheaper car, a coupé because the Americans were expected to outlaw open cars on the grounds of safety. This was introduced in 1975 as the 924 and soon superseded the 914.

Once the 924 was well under way, Porsche felt that they could concentrate on the new super-luxury machine, the 928, even though the 911 was still selling well – but surely it could not go on forever? The 928 was given a large (4.4 liter) V8 engine for the smoothest and most silent ability to meet what were expected to be severe emission regulations. It even got automatic transmission as part of its boulevard appeal – a feature that has never been popular on the 911. One of the strokes of genius that distinguished the 928 was the way in which bumpers were concealed behind flexible panels, in a far neater manner than the 'tacked-on' beams adopted by competitors.

So much choice…

The 928 was a superb vehicle and still is, but quite unlike the more highly tuned 911. As a result it has tended to appeal to customers who might have preferred a big saloon, rather than to the sports car fans, who continued to go for the traditional machinery.

Porsche did everything they could to promote the 924 and 928, but 911 sales remained firm. Development was concentrated on the front-engined cars, with the sportier 928S and the 924 Turbo, which had 928-style performance at two-thirds its price and half that of a 930. Then came the 924 Carrera in 1979, hoping to take over the mantle of the old 2.7 Carrera RS. Both new cars sold well, but they couldn't kill the 911, and subsequently the 924 Carrera was

made smoother to drive with a power unit that was virtually half that of the 928. The resultant 944 appealed especially to the American market. Porsche enthusiasts had the best of every world with so many models from which to choose.

Although technically good, the box-shaped 914 – pictured here in Volkswagen guise (below right) – was too stark and expensive to be a great success. The 924's cheeky appeal was emphasized, however, when its headlights were raised (bottom left) and it became a popular wheel-wagging attraction at race tracks when a series of events was organized to promote the model in 1978 (top left).

The raised-and-lowered headlight theme (top left) was carried over to the Porsche 928, which featured a rear spoiler on the S version (top center), and exceptionally neat flexible plastic panels concealing sturdy alloy beam bumpers (top right). This presented a clean and uncluttered profile in the more powerful and sophisticated series 4 version (below).

The Porsche 944 (above) is effectively a combination of the best aspects of the 924 (left) and the 928. It features the 924's low-cost bodyshell and economy equipment and the flexibility of the 928 engine with its four-cylinder unit

PICTURE CREDITS